LABORATORY PSYCHOLOGY

A Beginner's Guide

Edited by

Julia Nunn
City University

Psychology Press
a member of the Taylor & Francis group

Psychology Press Ltd, Publishers
27 Church Road
Hove
East Sussex, BN3 2FA
UK

British Library Cataloguing in Publication Data

A catalogue record for this book is available from the British Library

ISBN 0-86377-710-4 (hbk)
       0-86377-711-2 (pbk)

ISSN 1368-4558 (Cognitive Psychology: A Modular Course)

Cover illustration:
BLAKE, William, *Newton* (d1795/c1805) © Tate Gallery, London

Cover design by Joyce Chester
Printed and bound in the UK by TJ International Ltd, Padstow

Contents

Preface

When students opt for psychology they do so because of a desire to learn about how humans think, remember, and behave. It is a hybrid discipline which allows people to ponder the profound questions that have been worrying philosophers for years as well as do something that is meaningful in the contemporary world. These rather lofty ambitions are bluntly terminated when A-level and undergraduate students are faced with what may seem an overkill of statistics and methodology training. This tends to be a negative experience, as the methodologies, which characterise the scientific essence of psychology, are sometimes taught as if they are divorced from the reasons why students chose psychology.

The reason why methodology must play such a prominent role in teaching psychology is that the discipline is an empirical science, and one that has to deal with some truly difficult concepts in order to combat much so-called "commonsense" or folk psychology. From its inception as a scientific discipline, methodology in psychology has always been fundamental for progress. Some argue that methodology is the core of the discipline.

Experimental design is important enough to merit a book of its own, without statistics, that instead links methodology to a discussion of how psychologists can advance and reject theories about human behaviour. The objective of this book is to fulfil this role.

The book is intended primarily for first-year psychology undergraduates, although it is also appropriate for students on other courses being taught psychological methods. It incorporates exercises at the end of each chapter which could variously form the basis of a project, test comprehension of key concepts, or engender discussion.

The first four chapters lay the foundations of design in experimental psychology. The first chapter "Why does psychology need methodology?", justifies the prominent role given to methodology within the discipline. This chapter also counters some common criticisms of psychological research, thus paving the way for Chapters 2 and 3, which describe between-subjects and within-subject designs, respectively. Chapter 4 compares and contrasts the traditional experimental approach with that of the quasi-experimental, or correlational approach, concluding that the consequences of not recognising the value (and the limitations) of the quasi-experimental approach can be far-reaching.

The following three chapters discuss practical issues involved in running experiments. The first of these (Chapter 5) offers a comprehensive guide to the student researcher who wants to construct a good questionnaire, including a discussion of reliability and validity issues. The next chapter, entitled "People, materials, and situations" considers the basic tools of psychological research, while discussing both the theoretical problem of how a sample from a population is chosen, and offering useful hints on the practical issue of finding adequate populations from which to select participants. Chapter 7 considers ethical practice within psychological research, written in large part so that psychology students will be better able to anticipate ethical problems in their studies *before* they occur.

The final two chapters consider reporting and reading psychological papers. Chapter 8 details what should and should not be included in a laboratory report. We use our collective experience of marking numerous lab reports to highlight common errors and provide solutions. Finally, Chapter 9 describes the various elements of a journal article, including tips on how to get the best out of your journal reading.

Given that the statistical aspects of research methodology have been omitted, it seems wise to draw the reader's attention to a few books that could usefully accompany this text when analysing results:

Miller, S. (1984). *Experimental design and statistics* (2nd edn.). Methuen (Routledge).

Wright, D.B. (1997). *Understanding statistics: Introduction to statistics for the social sciences*. London: Sage Publications.

We have collected together a group of researchers with diverse backgrounds within cognitive psychology. The authorship "team" is CWORKS, the Cognitive Workshop of City University. The team comprises, in alphabetical order, Peter Ayton, John Gardiner, James Hampton, Liz Hellier, Zofia Kaminska, Julia Nunn, Ingrid Schoon, and Dan Wright. All CWORKS members are active researchers and lecture on methodological issues.

Julia Nunn
London, April 1997

Series Preface

Cognitive Psychology: A Modular Course, edited by Gerry Altmann and Susan E. Gathercole, aims to provide undergraduates with stimulating, readable, affordable brief texts by leading experts. Together with three other modular series, these texts will cover all the major topics studied at undergraduate level in psychology. The companion series are: Clinical Psychology, edited by Chris Brewin; Developmental Psychology, edited by Peter Bryant and George Butterworth; Social Psychology, edited by Miles Hewstone. The series will appeal to those who want to go deeper into the subject than the traditional textbook will allow, and base their examination answers, research, projects, assignments, or practical decisions on a clearer and more rounded appreciation of the research evidence.

Why does psychology need methodology? 1

Peter Ayton

T his chapter introduces the idea that psychology is a science that can and does—and indeed, *must*—pursue legitimate scientific methods to make progress. Unusually for a book of this kind some of it is written in the first person as it includes personal reminiscences; however the argument is not based on personal experience.

Aims

The aim of this chapter is to instil in the reader an understanding of the need for a scientific approach to the study of behaviour. The reader will be invited to consider the merits of the scientific approach as well as some of the challenges that this approach presents. After reading this chapter the reader should appreciate the need for scientific methodology in psychology as well as the potential for applying it.

Introduction

It is a fairly typical experience in the life of a psychology student to discover, shortly after they have embarked on the course, that it is not quite what they thought it might be. Although some new students have no really clear idea of what to expect (I had absolutely no idea), the image of human psychology is for many rather exciting, exotic, and mysterious. Somehow one expects to be dabbling in the psyche—using secret methods to reveal the hidden nature of human beings. In my view that's exactly what the methodology of psychology does enable one to do—nonetheless students often complain that laboratory and methodology courses are rather "dry" and technical. When I was an undergraduate psychology student one of my contemporaries complained to our tutor that they had chosen to study psychology because they: "…wanted to understand people—not to measure them doing 'silly things' and turn them into numbers…". At the time I was rather impressed by this argument and rather shocked by my tutor's characteristically robust response. He answered by suggesting that, if the student simply wanted to ponder the nature of people, then they might be better off reading the novels of Jane Austen or Tolstoy—but we were here to do science.

This sharp remark echoes the distinction that was identified by C.P. Snow in the 1950s according to which there are two separate cultures of thought that are attributable to the nature of educational attitudes. The culture of the literary intellectuals and the culture of the scientists view each other with mutual suspicion. According to Snow (1959) the position was then worsening; he could recall there had been a time when the two sides could at least manage "a frozen smile" but that they were by then incapable of communicating. My tutor and student colleague certainly didn't manage a smile of any description. Instead there was one of those awkward moments when two people discover that they have attitudes that will require more effort than they believe that the other is prepared (or able) to make to understand why they are wrong.

As an example of the difficulties that were produced by the separation between the two cultures, Snow pointed to the widespread ignorance of the second law of thermodynamics that was displayed—not just by the lay populace but by most contemporary intellectuals. It is as if laws of science are not considered relevant for understanding the world. As an illustrative example for psychology we could consider the widespread belief in astrology. It strikes me as indicative of a major problem somewhere that most people are apparently aware of the idea that there are twelve sorts of people whose personality is determined by their birth-date—but simultaneously quite unaware of any scientific theory of personality. Typically astrology proposes, for reasons that are never clear or even announced and with no reporting of evidence, that your behaviour and its consequences are determined by the movement of the planets. Meanwhile psychology struggles to specify and justify valid theories by testing them with carefully measured observations. Despite the self-critical nature of any science (scientists are, quite properly, forever criticising each other's theories) it seems that some people exclusively reserve their scepticism for scientific rather than unscientific claims. Belief in astrology as a means of predicting behaviour appears to be widespread; I have even met psychology students who are prepared to admit (often somewhat more defiantly than the term "admit" suggests) their belief in astrology! At the same time many students will wonder about the value of scientific approaches to the study of behaviour[1].

Is psychology a science?

All this talk of science and its merits and status requires some explanation. What exactly is science? There is no big mystery here, despite the rather portentous tone of some of the discussions of the nature of scientific enquiry. My dictionary defines science as systematic and formulated knowledge or the activity by which this knowledge is pursued based on observation, experiment, and induction. Astrologers do not seek to obtain knowledge by conducting systematic experiments. Astrologers use their methods simply to pronounce—they are not in the business of collecting observations to explore whether any theory they propose is false or in need of modification. As a consequence they cannot be considered as scientists. For the same reason we can also exclude graphologists, scientologists, and most psychoanalysts. But why shouldn't systematic knowledge about behaviour, including human behaviour, be pursued—and even discovered?

It is a fairly common task for the introductory student to be asked to write an essay discussing whether psychology is a science. I once discussed this habit with an eminent professor of psychology who told me that it was a mistake to ask students to write such an essay. "It would be the same as asking them to consider whether a chicken had lips," he said. "You have to consider what lips are, what chickens are and whether the former can be found with the latter. All this could be done of course and it could be a quite rigorous discussion, but to what end?" Perhaps such a debate (about psychology and science—not chickens and lips) is all very well for clarifying approaches to application of the scientific method in psychology but, plainly, psychology as practised is a science as it uses systematic methods for attempting to acquire knowledge.

Somehow, though, there is doubt that psychology really is a science. In Britain the main government body that funds psychological research has been required to change its name from the *Social Science Research Council* to the *Economic and Social Research Council*—science being neatly and quite deliberately excised from its heading. When the UK government had a Department of Education and Science (science was dropped from its brief recently) it did not consider psychology as a science subject at all, grouping it with such subjects as law and librarianship (Radford, 1982). Could these government perceptions be a symptom of Snow's two cultures? The notion that it might be useful to be scientific in order to understand people is often viewed with suspicion. But what is the alternative?

The style of the early part of my science education invited the conclusion that all the world's mysteries had been largely solved by the end of the nineteenth century and my job as a student was simply to learn what had been discovered. When we conducted experiments in physics, chemistry, or biology they were usually in the nature of demonstrations of principles and effects that were considered well established truths. In a sense it was more like science history than science *per se*. All around the walls of my school science laboratory were pictures of eminent Victorian scientists—usually men with long grey beards—who glowered down as we struggled with Bunsen burners and test-tubes in our efforts to demonstrate what was known to be true. Sometimes our experiments "didn't work" and we were left feeling incompetent (unless the failed experiment was conducted by the teacher in which case we were jubilant).

Never, as I recall, did we conduct an experiment that we had devised ourselves in order to test the validity of a new idea that might add to the existing stock of knowledge about the world. No doubt this is due, at least in part, to the fact that there was a lot to learn about the relationship between scientific theories and laboratory phenomena. Given the huge amount of scientific knowledge in the traditional sciences, simply learning about what was well established took years. Nonetheless I was left with the impression that science chiefly involved the application of well understood principles. Those grey-bearded faces on the walls seemed to be saying that they had solved all the world's mysteries and it was simply my job to learn what they had discovered. It never occurred to me until years later when I studied psychology that science was an ongoing and very much alive process of acquiring and testing new ideas.

In terms of creating the impression that all is solved, psychology is perhaps obliged to be a little more modest in its approach; for a science that is officially only a little over a century old there may be relatively rather little to serve up in the way of impressive demonstrations of well established truths—although there are some. The very first experiments that students will carry out are usually conducted in order to reveal well established reliable phenomena. Before very long however, students will be prompted to devise their own experiments testing their own hypotheses. The nature of psychology invites people to challenge and extend the current state of knowledge. Whereas early laboratory experiments may consist of demonstrations, fairly soon the psychology student will, or should, feel encouraged to embark on their own train of thought and attempt to do something new. In order to do this, though, one does need to know how to go about acquiring knowledge.

Methods for acquiring knowledge

In his defence of empirical psychology Broadbent (1973) identified three possible methods for acquiring knowledge. First, one might assume that one could just wander about the world observing as you go—more or less at random—and the facts of nature will inevitably compel you to induce certain generalisations. This no doubt happens to some degree (perhaps this is where astrology came from) but it is not recommended as a method for obtaining valid theories. In the first place, unguided intuition is not always reliable; people can come to conclusions that would not be supported by an objective perusal of the facts. Enormous feelings of confidence about an explanation are no guarantee of its viability—as psychological research has established (cf. McClelland & Bolger, 1994). Furthermore, it is rather limited as a means of obtaining the observations in the first place. As the rest of this book teaches, it is desirable to structure one's approach to the measurement of phenomena in order to be able to explain them. In order to measure *systematically* it is often necessary to create particular conditions where measurements will be unaffected by interfering factors. It is this requirement to be systematic that results in the formulation of methodology for collecting useful data by, for example, conducting experiments that are specially designed and controlled so as to enable clear measures to be made. In order to gather observations selectively one has to adopt a strategy for doing so. This strategy—the methodology—will vary according to the circumstances that one is dealing with, but, as this book teaches, there are certain tricks of the trade.

The second method identified by Broadbent is what is referred to as the hypothetico-deductive approach. This approach is systematic. Here one proposes a theory, predicts the consequences from it and organises the collection of observations selectively so as to determine the truth or falsity of the predictions from the theory. The hypothetico-deductive method is a popular model for psychological investigations. Most scientists do not wander about observing at random and they are also fond of pointing out that one can never prove the truth of a theory but only disprove it. Thus, if you make clear predictions from a theory you have specified a means by which it might be shown to be false. If the theory survives the empirical test then one can feel that much more confident in the truth of the theory—or at least one has shown that, for the experimental situation studied, it works. It is easy to see this approach as a sort of competition for survival of the fittest. A theory that is testable will only survive if it successfully accounts for the observations used to test it. Thus good theories would survive scientific test and bad theories would either have to be adapted to pass the test or be discarded. By this method science could be seen as progressing on an evolutionary basis.

There is another way however—the third method identified by Broadbent. What is known as the Bayesian approach[2] advocates that one should not consider just a single theory but consider what alternatives there might be. We can think of it as a market-place of ideas with competition among a number of alternative theories. Advocates of the Bayesian approach have criticised simple hypothesis testing on the grounds that psychologists have sometimes tested their favourite theories by making predictions that could also be predicted by a number of other rival theories. If a number of different theories make the same prediction as the one that you have set out to test, then there will be no progress in determining the best theory. Moreover, if the prediction turns out to be inconsistent with the facts—i.e. wrong—then you will be left literally at a loss to explain what has been observed.

When faced with this outcome I have seen students attempt to explain away the results of their experiments. For example, they will often argue that perhaps the subjects in their experiment didn't properly understand the instructions, or perhaps the room was too noisy and distracted them, or perhaps they weren't motivated to attend in the first place. Now all of these are legitimate possibilities but, of course, one should also at least consider the possibility that the theory that led to the predictions is simply wrong; perhaps people just don't behave in the manner implied by the theory. In fact if we are not prepared to consider this possibility then there is very little point in going to the trouble of conducting the experiment in the first place.

The idea that the scientific theory might be wrong can take some getting used to. After the shock of discovering what psychology is like and learning to cope with methodology there is for many students another far more traumatic shock. Psychologists are not like the men with grey beards in the pictures—they are people who don't know all the answers! This can create a good deal of discomfort for students who have been taught to expect that science is full of answers and reliable truths. Sometimes, as a consequence, it will be tempting to dismiss psychology as not a true science. However, if one sees it as a challenge to contribute to the progress of the subject rather than be despondent about its (lack of) achievements to date, the result can be quite exhilarating. Something needs to be done and proper methods of enquiry must be pursued in order to do it.

Many's the time I have heard a student complain that their experiment didn't "work". But in a sense all experiments "work" because everything always happens how it "should"—how could it not? However, the theories, or the predictions, or the way in which the predictions are measured and tested, may not be valid. I suspect that the basis for the "it didn't work" complaint (particularly for its typically despondent tone) may be a hangover from the perception of laboratory science as consisting of a series of demonstrations of what is known to happen for reasons that are known to be true (those pictures of Victorian gentlemen scientists again come to mind). In fact the state of the science of psychology (and, in truth, the other sciences as well) is much more exciting than that. To a very large extent we simply don't know how things happen—that is why we are engaged in science in the first place—we are trying to find out. Trying to find out why things happen as they do is not easy—in psychology, for reasons considered in the next section, it may be much harder. The process of conducting scientific psychology entails much critical questioning and rigorous examination of theory, method, and conclusion. But that is not a reason to abandon the effort to engage in scientific psychology; in fact it is a very good reason why psychology must apply scientific standards with even greater effort.

Some objections to experimental psychology

It cannot be denied that there have been many thoughtful and highly influential criticisms of experimental methods in psychology—many of them coming from psychologists themselves. In this section I will briefly consider two of these objections and what can be said or done to counter or appease them.

Scientific psychology cannot be applied to the real world

When one goes about the process of systematically collecting observations of behaviour under controlled conditions one often reduces the complexity of human action to its much simpler constituent processes. This piecemeal approach to the study of behaviour enables psychologists to gain a measure of control. In conducting a laboratory experiment, for example, psychologists quite deliberately create an artificial situation which is an attempt to model some aspect of the real world. For example, research into the effects of alcohol on driving was not conducted using subjects driving a real car but instead used a driving simulator. Aside from the ethical problems involved in administering alcohol to car drivers, the fact that it is only a model of reality and not the real-world situation means that it is possible to obtain some systematic measurements of performance which will be uncontaminated by other variables. For example, with a simulator one could perfectly control the weather and traffic conditions, the nature of any hazards, and the way the car responded to the brakes and steering. One might also try to ensure that none of the participants in the experiment was sleep-deprived or taking any medical treatments or extremely short-sighted or very old.

However, one criticism of this approach to experimental psychology is that for the very reason that measurements can be systematically made they will be unreliable for generalising to the real world where many factors may affect the behaviour being measured in complex ways (cf. Chapanis, 1967). One worry with testing driving performance in a simulator is that the drivers may not experience the situation as realistic. If you know that you cannot really crash the car then you might not concentrate on the task in the same way or experience much of the stress that real drivers encounter. This might in turn lead you to drive in a far riskier fashion than you would normally. Notice that people in amusement arcades are willing to pay to enjoy the pleasure of "driving" very fast (and usually crashing) in a simulator. Moreover, if we select the participants for the experiment, in the hope of avoiding individual differences affecting the results, then, by the same token, we risk over-generalisation. For example, a small amount of alcohol might not particularly affect the driving performance of a 25-year-old in good health with normal vision, but might be quite devastating to an elderly individual with short-sight who is taking certain medications to treat persistent migraines.

The number of factors that may influence the behaviour of interest is potentially immense. The environment that we live in is psychologically very complex and full of many interacting influences on our behaviour. For example, Broadbent (1963) found that the combined effects of different sources of stress such as noise, sleeplessness, and high temperatures sometimes make performance worse than if just one stress is present, but sometimes partially cancel each other out. This sort of complexity can also render observational and questionnaire studies misleadingly simplistic (cf. Proshansky, 1972).

The point is a reasonable one and no doubt a good deal of psychological research is vulnerable to the criticism. Nonetheless, it is not the case that the point invalidates any conclusion arrived at through experimentation. First we should note that the evidence for the problem is obtainable from psychological research itself; Broadbent's (1963) research successfully determined that there were complex interactions between different stressors by the careful use of psychological experimentation. Laboratory research can be designed to accommodate and measure complex interactions. Indeed, one of the strengths of the scientific approach is that one can develop research so as to measure the impact of more and more previously untracked variables. Many experiments that have been formulated to test a particular hypothesis can and have been applied successfully to a broad range of different situations where different factors might have affected the outcome of the results. A further point that can be made is that psychologists seeking to explain some behaviour that occurs in the real world need not learn from the results of laboratory experiments alone. If an experimentally formulated solution fails to prove successful when applied back to the real world, psychologists are still in a position to reconsider and redesign an experiment to find the correct solution.

It is also worth pointing out that this type of problem is in no way confined to psychological research. Other fields of scientific enquiry suffer these sorts of difficulties without triggering any sort of a crisis as to whether they are sciences. For example when testing the effects of chemical additives in food, food scientists typically do not test for the combined effects of a large number of additives. Additives are usually tested individually—any interactions that may occur between two harmless substances to create a dangerous one would not be detected. Medical researchers are now seriously concerned about the effects on health of patients taking large numbers of different drugs at the same time (*New Scientist*, 1996). "Drug cocktail" effects are a serious risk as there may well be a large number of unknown interactions between drugs of which doctors are unaware.

Plainly, in any field where there are a large number of factors that may affect what is being studied, care should be taken. It is important to note, however, that there are means by which care can be taken; replications of studies in different and diverse situations should be performed.

Scientific psychology deliberately avoids the real world

A common starting point for many fields of psychological research has been some practical real-world problem. One famous example is the field of research in psychology known as signal detection theory. This started when people tried to understand the behaviour of human beings operating systems such as radar or sonar where the operator had to look or listen for infrequent signals. This research progressed when psychologists devised tasks that they thought modelled the sort of environment that they were interested in. However, fairly quickly the work developed in such a way that it was claimed that the findings of the research were not relevant to any monitoring problems (Chapanis, 1967).

Similar points have been made by other authors for different fields of research in psychology. For example, Newell (1972) argued that psychologists might purport to be interested in a "grand issue" such as how language is learned or how memory works, but they tend to work by evaluating behaviour at a very low level. So although you might claim to be interested in how memory works, you might actually spend your time analysing a series of rather tiny effects such as why people remember words at the beginning or end of a list better than those in the middle of the list (the serial-position effect). Newell was rather pessimistic that this approach would lead to progress, arguing that: "you can't play 20 questions with nature and win".

Neisser (1978) has also taken exception to this pattern of behaviour in psychology and pointed out that a memory researcher revealing his occupation to a non-psychologist friend would be quite likely to be asked questions about all sorts of interesting phenomena that he would be unable to say anything about. For example, his friend might mention his Aunt's prodigious memory for poetry, his failure to remember appointments, and why he found it so hard to remember people's names. Neisser thought that this failure was inexcusable given that memory research had been proceeding for 100 years.

More recently, in a paper eye-catchingly entitled "The real world: what good is it?", Fischhoff (1996) has argued that the laboratory tasks that were created as surrogates for complicated real-world situations can take on lives of their own. When that happens, Fischhoff argues, scientists become fascinated with the nuances of variations within that little world. As a result their theoretical accounts end up with little place for phenomena that could not be observed there, and extrapolations to other settings may require large doses of conjecture (or leaps of faith).

Such complaints about the way psychologists appear to forget that they ought to be trying to provide useful accounts of real behaviour are, I think, useful reprimands. They suggest that psychology is not inherently unable to be useful, but that psychologists have a tendency to avoid being so. To some degree I suspect that this can be attributed to plain laziness. It is often easier to conduct research that explores a laboratory effect than it is to effectively answer questions about some real mystery of psychology. My student friend who was attracted to psychology because they "…wanted to understand people—not to measure them doing 'silly things' and turn them into numbers…" might even feel a little vindicated.

I would also add in their defence that psychologists do seem able to respond to such criticisms. In the years since Newell's and Neisser's papers for example there have been a number of studies of the practical aspects of memory, and theories have been developed to explain such phenomena as the difficulties in remembering names (e.g. Cohen, 1990). There has also been a noticeable development of journals devoted to specifically applied topics of research (e.g. *Applied Cognitive Psychology*; *Journal of Experimental Psychology: Applied*). The problem is doubtless real, but the solution is often heavily hinted at by those making the complaint.

Conclusions

in this chapter I have argued that psychology has to be pursued scientifically in order to make progress. That means employing systematic methodology. A number of challenges for and criticisms of scientific psychology have been considered. While some of these criticisms and challenges must be taken very seriously, none of them can be held to invalidate the attempt to pursue scientific explanations for behaviour. To those who remain sceptical about the scientific approach to psychology we can reasonably ask of them just one question: What alternative is there?

References

Bayes, T. (1763). An essay towards solving a problem in the doctrine of chances. *Philosophical Transactions of the Royal Society, 53,* 370–418.

Broadbent, D.E. (1963). Differences and interactions between stresses. *Quarterly Journal of Experimental Psychology, 15,* 205–211.

Broadbent, D.E. (1973). *In defence of empirical psychology.* London: Methuen.

Chapanis, A. (1967). The relevance of laboratory studies to practical situations. *Ergonomics, 10,* 557–577.

Cohen, G. (1990). Why is it difficult to put names to faces? *British Journal of Psychology, 81,* 287–297

Fischhoff, B. (1996). The real world: What good is it? *Organizational Behavior and Human Decision Processes, 65,* 232–248.

Mayo, J., White, O., & Eysenck, H.J. (1978). An empirical study of the relation between astrological factors and personality. *Journal of Social Psychology, 105,* 229–236.

McClelland, A.G.R., & Bolger, F. (1994). The calibration of subjective probabilities: Theories and models 1980–1994. In G. Wright and P. Ayton (Eds.), *Subjective probability.* Chichester, UK: Wiley.

Neisser, U. (1978). Memory: What are the important questions? In M.M. Gruneberg, P.E. Morris, & R.N. Sykes (Eds.), *Practical aspects of memory.* London: Academic Press.

Newell, A. (1972). You can't play 20 questions with nature and win: Projective comments on the papers of this symposium. In W.G. Chase (Ed.), *Visual information processing.* New York: Academic Press.

New Scientist (1996). "Drug cocktails have hidden risk". 21 September, p.13.

Pawlik, K., & Buse, L. (1979). Selbst Attribuirung als differentiell-psychologische Moderator-variabele: Nachprüfung und Erklärung von Eysenck's Astrologie Personlichkeits-korrelationen. [Self attribution as a differential psychological moderator variable: Check and explanations of Eysenck's Astrology–Personality correlations.] *Zeitschrift für Sozialpsychologie, 10,* 54–69.

Phillips, D.P., Ruth, T.E., & Wagner, L.M. (1993). Psychology and survival. *The Lancet, 342,* 1142–1145.

Proshansky, H.M. (1972). Methodology in environmental psychology: Problems and issues. *Human Factors, 14,* 451–460.

Radford, J. (1982). Review of Beer, J. "Experiments in psychology: A workbook for students". *Perception, 11,* 497–498.

Snow, C.P. (1959). *The two cultures and the scientific revolution: Rede Lecture*. Cambridge: Cambridge University Press.

Van Rooij, J.J.F. (1994). Introversion and extraversion: Astrology versus psychology. *Personality and Individual Differences*, 16, 985–988.

Notes

1. Actually there are a number of psychological studies that have attempted to scientifically evaluate the extent to which there is any validity for astrological predictions. One proposition in astrology suggests that people born with the sun in a so-called "positive" sign of the zodiac (Aries, Gemini, Leo, Libra, Sagittarius, Aquarius) are more extraverted, while those born with the sun in a "negative" sign (Taurus, Cancer, Virgo, Scorpio, Capricorn, Pisces) tend to be introverted. A number of studies have found that this prediction is borne out; those with a positive sign are more extravert than those with a negative sign (Mayo, White & Eysenck, 1978; Pawlik & Buse, 1979; Van Rooij, 1993). However, this effect can be explained as due to self-attribution; people who know their sunsign may attribute to themselves the personality characteristics assigned to the sign. Consistent with this interpretation Pawlik and Buse (1979) and Van Rooij (1993) found that the effect only held for those people who had astrological knowledge. A rather more disturbing demonstration of the effects of belief in astrology is reported by Phillips, Ruth and Wagner (1993). They studied the age of death of a large sample of Chinese Americans and compared it with the age of death of a large sample of white Americans. They found that the Chinese Americans, but not white Americans, die significantly earlier than normal if they have a combination of disease and birth year which Chinese astrology and medicine consider ill-fated. The more strongly the sample was attached to Chinese traditions the more years of life were lost. The effect applied to nearly all the major causes of death studied. The authors argue that this effect is at least in part due to psychosomatic processes. Belief in astrology is not just unwarranted, it can also be bad for your health.

2. The Reverend Thomas Bayes was a mathematician and non-conformist minister who preached in Tunbridge Wells in the eighteenth century. Two years after his death a paper on probability attributed to him was published (Bayes, 1763). The ideas

in that paper eventually gave rise to what is now known as Bayes' theorem which is a mathematical procedure that can be used as a means for determining the relative credibility of different hypotheses in the light of evidence.

The between-subjects experiment

2

James Hampton

Between-subjects vs within-subject designs

The title of this and the next chapter relate to a basic distinction in the way in which experiments can be designed. In the simplest possible terms, where the behaviour of two (or more) different groups of people is compared, this is a *between-subjects* design, whereas when a comparison is made of the behaviour of the same group of people under different conditions, this is a *within-subject* design. In the present chapter, we will be concerned with the first of these two experimental methods. First, however, we will present a brief account of scientific methods and how they are applied in experimental psychology.

Aims

Modern psychology, as it has been pursued in the last hundred years, is a branch of science. Like many sciences it has many different forms. As a practical science it is applied in clinical, educational, and business settings. As a pure science it has undergone an extremely rapid expansion in the past few decades, as more and more is learned about the fundamental workings of the mind and the brain. The focus of this book is the application of scientific methods to the study of human psychology. In this chapter we aim to:

- Explain the basic processes involved in any science.
- Discuss their particular application to studying the human mind.
- Introduce the notion of the "ideal" experiment.

- Explain how to construct a between-subjects experiment.
- Explain the importance of statistical methods for assessing the results of psychology experiments.

Understanding, predicting, controlling

Much has been written about the nature and logic of the scientific method, and the special place of scientific knowledge in modern culture. Controversy still abounds in the philosophical literature over just why science should be so successful, and whether society is justified in according scientific findings such respect. For our purposes, we do not need to stray into these deep waters, but we do need to have a clear view of what the scientific method entails, in order to be reassured that the knowledge we gain from research in psychology will have the guarantee of validity and objectivity (and hence respectability) that the scientific method, when properly applied, bestows on its results. What follows is a highly idealised account of scientific practice, which would probably not be recognised by historians of science. Science was once a branch of philosophy, and the reliance of theories on empirical observation and experiment is a relatively recent innovation. The reason for presenting an idealised version is to explain the logic underlying the process, rather than to paint a picture of the messy business of how science actually evolved.

Science begins with observation. We look at the world around us and notice things happening, and ask ourselves the questions "how" and "why". What we are looking for as an answer to these questions may involve explanations at different levels—from an explanation of the mechanics (the how) of some observed object of study—to an explanation of why the observed phenomenon arises on some occasions but not others, and what causal links it has to previous and subsequent events. We begin then by identifying a phenomenon and by wanting to know more about it.

The first stage after noticing the phenomenon should then be to observe it more closely and more systematically. Suppose the object of our study were the occurrence of hooliganism among football supporters. The curious psychologist/social scientist would begin their study by collecting as many observations as possible—attending matches, listening and talking to supporters, collecting statistics about the incidence of trouble at different places and on different occasions. Alternatively if the phenomenon was the apparent occurrence of false memories of traumatic events in childhood, one could begin by interviewing individuals with such memories, investigating the validity of the memories through historical evidence where it exists, and building up a large collection of observations of similar cases.

With this process, two developments can occur. First, new phenomena or facts may emerge. When we are faced with a large body of observations, we may often observe patterns in the data. With the advantage of statistical software programs, we can in fact do a "trawl" through data bases looking for such patterns. This process is known as "induction"—the development of a generalisation that captures an observed pattern in the data. (Philosophers of science are also concerned about the validity of induction as a method for arriving at objective knowledge, as there are an infinite number of generalisations that will fit any given pattern of data, and the reasons for choosing one over another are far from clear.)

The second development is the refinement of the ways in which our observations are made. In many sciences, improvements in methods of observation have been absolutely critical to the progress of the science. Advances in astronomy have depended heavily on advances in the technology of telescopes, while advances in cell biology have similarly depended on ever more sophisticated ways of preparing tissue samples, marking particular parts of the cell, separating out relevant structures, and so forth. In fact the more our knowledge advances, so the more our methods for discovery about the phenomenon can advance. For psychology, there has been a similar advance over the last few decades in methods of observation and measurement. Often the discovery of new methods (sometimes known as "paradigms") and new phenomena have gone hand-in-hand.

Once systematic and reliable observations have been established, then the scientist is ready to begin forming theories of what gives rise to the phenomenon being studied. (In real life, it is unlikely that scientists would always wait to form theories until observations have been established. Historically, there have probably always been theories of one kind or another, and the way in which observations are made and the reasons for making them are often dictated by those theories and what phenomena they define to be relevant. However for the sake of exposition, I am suggesting that scientific theories are logically preceded by systematic observations.)

Exactly where theories come from is another of the mysteries of the philosophy of science, and is a field of psychological study in its own right. A theory is a statement of a general principle, which as applied to the particular setting being observed can account for the regularities in the observations. Theories in psychology can take many different forms, from highly detailed and specific mechanistic models of how a part of the nervous system functions (as in for example the processing of information by the retina of the eye), to the highly abstract (and sometimes frustratingly vague) theories found in inter-personal psychology. The important part of an explanatory theory is that it should be predictive. This is to say that not only can the theory account for all the known facts, regularities, or observed phenomena in its domain of application, but it can also predict the existence of new results that have yet to be found. This is as true of psychology as of any other form of science, and it is the only true test of a scientific theory. Constructing a theory to explain known facts is known as *post hoc* explanation—explaining "after the fact". Such explanations may be more or less convincing, depending on a range of other factors such as their plausibility given other knowledge of the world, and the number of competing explanations that can be imagined. Where a theory scores over others is when it directs the scientist to perform new experiments, and it correctly predicts the results.

Perhaps the most convincing argument for the correctness of a theory is when it allows scientists not only to predict the outcome of experiments, but also to control events in the world. The success of the microbiological theory of disease is hard to challenge given the degree to which its application has allowed doctors to rid the world of many infectious diseases.

When a science reaches a state of some maturity, then there will be many cases where there are alternative rival theories of a particular phenomenon. It is in this situation that the use of experiments is most valuable, because by careful selection of the experimental conditions, it should be possible to devise *critical experiments* in which the predictions made by alternate theories are at odds with each other. By running the experiment, it is in principle then possible to tell which theory is correct (if any). In science, theorists may propose, but nature disposes through experimental results. In principle, just one incorrect prediction is sufficient to falsify a theory, as scientists require that a correct theory should have no countervailing evidence (a view put forward by Popper, 1972). Ideally then, a scientist with a precious new theory should immediately set about trying to find evidence to falsify it, because logically speaking a theory may make endless correct predictions but still be false. Progress demands that we seek to falsify our theories, and that we only retain those that stand up to this severe test. In practice this ideal is rarely found. It is more common that different groups of scientists espousing rival theories busy themselves running experiments that may falsify those of the opposing group. It can also be argued that there is considerable merit in performing experiments that may provide verification of the predictions of a theory—particularly when the theory is in its early stages of development.

SUMMARY

- Science starts with observations.
- When systematic observations are made, inductive generalisations may emerge.
- Theories are abstract general principles which account for the observations.
- Theories are successful if they predict new results not previously observed.
- Competing theories are often tested using critical experiments.

The ideal experiment

We have seen how once a scientist begins to get an idea of what is going on, possible alternative accounts may arise. It is at this point that the urge to "tinker with nature" takes over, and the scientist starts to plan an experiment. An experiment involves asking a question of nature—what will happen if I do such-and-such? It differs critically from mere observation in the fact that the experimenter *chooses* to create a particular condition and to observe its outcome. ("Condition" is a technical term here, which means a particular set of circumstances in which an experimental observation is made). By repeating the experimental manipulation and noting that the outcome is generally the same, the scientist can then come to frame a law about nature of the form "every time I do X, the result tends to be Y". (We say "tends to be", because generally the results of experiments are probabilistic rather than certain.) Other scientists can then repeat the experiment and confirm for themselves the validity of the law.

There is one clear caveat to this story, which is that all relevant conditions of the experiment have to be exactly the same each time if the result is to come out the same. This is known as the *ceteris paribus* or "other things being equal" condition. The problem of course is that no-one can tell beforehand (or afterwards) what all the relevant conditions should be that must be held constant in order to successfully replicate an experiment. General common-sense may

Psychology occupies a peculiar position in the ranks of human knowledge. Few of us would claim to know much about cell biology or the formation of mountain ranges, but in a certain sense we are all of us experts in psychology. The evolution of man as a social species, heavily dependent on others of our group for our survival, has led us to evolve a highly developed ability to guess the thoughts, motives, and reactions of others of our species. So when psychologists start to address a particular issue of thought or behaviour, there is always this "naive" or folk psychology against which our efforts are measured. Compared with many sciences, there is a greater tendency for psychology to be accused of proving the obvious—for example that forgetting increases with time, or that people perform badly at tasks if they become too stressed or over-aroused. We cannot begin our observations in a "theory-neutral" way, because we already possess a solid body of implicit folk psychology with its own ways of explaining the phenomena we are studying. Fortunately for the science of psychology, researchers have been able to discover a great number of striking and counter-intuitive findings, with which to answer their critics. (Newton and Galileo had similar problems combating the folk theories of physics and astronomy of their days.) However, the influence of folk psychology on both the concepts used by psychologists (for example "intelligence" or "learning"), and on the perceived relevance and interest of results should not be underestimated.

dictate that performance in a memory task is likely to be affected by aspects of the individual's mood or arousal state or by aspects of the way in which the material to be learned is presented. It may also dictate that performance will be unaffected by whether the individual had fried or boiled eggs for breakfast, or by the current state of the stock market. However there are indefinitely many other variables that *might* affect performance, and no way of testing or controlling for them all. It is worth pointing out that these problems are common in other sciences (for example in biology), but are especially prevalent in psychology. The human central nervous system is one of the most complex systems imaginable, and its behaviour is open to influence from a wide range of internal and external factors. The problem for the experimenter then is to try to show that performing some manipulation on this system causes a systematic and reliable effect on its behaviour. To show this, it is necessary:

(a) to manipulate the system effectively;
(b) to measure the effect sensitively; and
(c) to keep all other relevant conditions the same.

Each of these aspects of an experiment pose particular problems for psychologists. We will consider each in turn.

Experimental manipulations

When an experimenter chooses to vary some aspect of the experimental task, in order to observe its effect, what is manipulated is known as the *independent variable*. It is independent because it depends only on the whim of the experimenter—that is, it is the start of a causal chain which has only the experimenter's choice in the matter as its triggering cause. The effect that is measured is likewise called the *dependent variable* because in this case the value of the measured variable is hypothesised to *depend* on the experimental conditions. If the experiment is successful then in effect the dependent variable depends on the manipulation of the independent variable. It is as though the independent variable were a lever that can be pulled and which reliably produces predictable results in the dependent variable. Through manipulation of the independent variable, the experimenter can (to some significant extent) *control* and predict the behaviour of the dependent variable. Learning how to control the world is a first step in learning how it works.

When planning an experiment yourself, one of the first problems you will face is deciding just how to define or set up your independent variable. If you hypothesise that listening to cool jazz helps people to think more clearly, then you need to define what exactly counts as cool jazz. Similarly, if you hypothesise that when people are relaxed they are better able to perceive emotions in others, then you need to find a way of *manipulating* how relaxed the person is within the scope of your experimental procedure. An important point that is not immediately obvious to many students is that all experiments should contain at least *two* conditions. If you wish to show that cool jazz clarifies one's thinking, then you have to be able to compare the jazz condition with something else. Otherwise how will you know that the thinking has become any clearer? This comparison condition is a vital part of experimentation, and is usually known as the *control condition*. Ideally the control condition is as similar to the experimental condition in every way possible *except for* the manipulation of the independent variable. You then know that if the experiment works, it is for the right reasons, and not because of some other systematic way in which the groups differed.

Independent variables then are constituted by the difference between your experimental condition and your control condition. The extent to which this difference really does reflect the theoretical construct that you have tried to build into it will determine the validity of the experiment. For example if your hypothesis states that "relaxation aids the perception of emotion", you have an implicit theoretical construct of "relaxation". To manipulate relaxation, you will need two conditions, where the only difference between them is the degree of relaxation of the participants. If your choice of manipulation fails to convince other scientists that you have truly varied the theoretical construct, then your results will be equally unconvincing. For example if you decide to take as your two conditions listening to country and western music as opposed to revising for statistics examinations, other researchers might argue that this is not a clean manipulation of the "relaxation" construct, and so might not consider that your experiment would prove anything at all about the effects of relaxation *per se*.

Another important point to bear in mind when choosing how to define your independent variable is the degree to which broader and less interesting accounts of your results might be possible. Let us suppose that I compare performance on a reasoning task for two groups of participants, one performing in silence and the other performing while listening to a background of Miles Davis's *Blue Moods*. Further suppose that the latter group do significantly better at the task. I may wish to claim that jazz aids mental reasoning, and this was indeed the hypothesis I set out to test. But of course the effect observed may not be specific to jazz. It may work equally well for Mozart, for Stravinsky, or for the Sex Pistols. It may in fact work just as strongly if the sound is that of a burglar alarm or of a thunderstorm.

Identifying the independent variable: What has actually been manipulated?

A classic study that showed the problems that may arise with independent variables was an experiment conducted at the Hawthorne factory of Western Electric, outside Chicago. The researchers thought that perhaps an increase in the lighting levels would improve productivity. When lighting levels were increased, productivity did indeed go up. However at the end of the experimental period, when the lights were turned back down to their original levels, productivity went up again! The original conclusion that productivity depended on lighting level was incorrect. Rather, it appeared that productivity responded to any change in environmental conditions—the workers were simply responding to the attention that was being paid to them (see Roethlisberger & Dickson, 1964).

The problem here is one of identifying the *boundary conditions* of an effect. My beautiful theory that the logical structure of jazz improvisation stimulates parts of the brain that are involved in reasoning is replaced by a rather dull conclusion that any auditory input leads to improved performance (perhaps it keeps the participants awake).

Having identified an experimental result (in this case that jazz improves reasoning), the careful researcher needs to continue to push the choice of the experimental and control conditions to identify at what point the effect ceases to be produced. It is for this reason that most research projects involve a *series* of related experiments, mapping out the territory in terms of the possible ways in which the independent variable can be manipulated. In the case where a research project is of limited scope, you should nonetheless be aware of the possibility that your independent variable is working for reasons other than the specific theory that you had in mind, and qualify your conclusions accordingly.

SUMMARY

- Theories are tested experimentally by constructing an independent variable.
- Independent variables can be thought of as being constituted by the difference between an experimental and a control condition.
- How an independent variable is constructed always involves assumptions that may be incorrect.
- The external validity of the experiment depends on the independent variable being a valid reflection of the theoretical construct.
- A number of different control groups may be necessary to pin down exactly what aspect of the independent variable is actually producing the result.

Measuring the effect

Just as choice of the independent variable needs careful thought, so does choosing the dependent variable. Primarily the same reasons apply as before. Your experiment will only be taken seriously as evidence concerning some theory if both the independent variable you manipulate and the dependent variable you measure are of direct relevance to that theory. There is always a process of translation between a theoretical proposition (for example: arousal increases during the day, deeper comprehension of material leads to longer-lasting memories) and the specific ways in which it is measured in an experiment. In mature sciences, the theory itself may dictate the way in which the dependent variable should be measured. Thus the measurement of temperature in physics experiments is itself dictated by the theoretical concept of temperature. In biology indirect measures are frequently employed, as when levels of an antibody are used to indicate the degree of an infection. In psychology we rarely have such theoretical precision to guide us in our choice of dependent variable, and we must rely on common sense to guide us. As a rule cognitive psychologists aim to keep their dependent variables simple and direct. For example, how many words were recalled, how many errors were made, how fast was the response, how accurate was the perception.

Just as with the independent variable, a careful researcher will consider using a range of different dependent variables to establish the theoretical significance and generality of an effect. For example a theoretical concept such as the strength of a memory trace can be measured in a number of ways—through likelihood of recall of the memory, through the ability to discriminate the true memory from other similar items that were not actually experienced, through the

---

Dependent variables based on psychometric scales

In areas of psychology involving personality and social behaviour there has been a rush to devise scales and tests to measure different aspects of the individual. Thus we have depression inventories, personality scales, intelligence, attitude and creativity tests, as well as measures of people's sexual preferences and gender identity. Use of such scales is increasingly common in student research projects (although it is quite rare to find them used as dependent variables in *experimental* designs). The student wishing to use one needs to bear several factors in mind:

(a) Scales are often developed by researchers for use with particular target populations. If your population is markedly different, the reliability of the scale (the degree to which it provides a pure measure undiluted by random noise) may become quite low. Check the reliability of the scale before drawing any conclusions.

(b) The degree to which the scale is a valid reflection of the theoretical construct depends only on the face validity of the items in the scale (and not on the prestige of its originator!). You should only use a scale if you are happy that each scale item is a fair measure of the theoretical construct you want to measure.

(c) Many scales are copyrighted, and the authors require a substantial fee for their use. Check with your supervisor before photocopying and distributing questionnaires. You may be infringing copyright law.

speed and confidence with which people can identify the item as previously experienced and reject lures, and through the ease with which they can relearn the same material once it has been forgotten. If an independent variable can be shown to affect all of these measures, then it is more likely to be truly affecting the strength of the memory trace itself, rather than some more trivial aspect of one particular measure. This procedure is known as the use of *converging measures*. Likewise, to the extent that all these dependent measures respond alike to different independent variables, then the theoretical construct of memory trace strength receives greater validation.

To illustrate the importance of this point, consider again the influence of cool jazz on reasoning that we used as an example before. When discussing independent variables, I pointed out how one would need to check that the effect was actually specific to cool jazz and not just general to any kind of noise. The same question of specificity can also be asked of the dependent variable. Is it just reasoning that is affected, or is the effect more general? If you were to find that not just reasoning but also typing, driving, dart throwing, and ability to do mental arithmetic were all improved in the experimental condition, then the kind of explanation you would offer would again have to be much more general. Clearly the most interesting results involve very specific independent variables producing very specific effects. If the results are too general, then they tend to be uninteresting, being merely examples of general principles such as arousal, fatigue, or degree of motivation.

SUMMARY

- The choice of dependent variable also involves assumptions.
- Try to keep your dependent variable simple and direct.
- Where possible consider using several dependent variables to provide converging measures of the effectiveness of the independent variable.
- Check whether the effects generated are specific to the particular dependent variable as predicted, or whether they may be more general effects influencing a broad range of measures.

Keeping other things constant

In an ideal world, each experiment would have a well motivated independent variable, and everything else would be exactly the same between conditions. In practice, psychology falls far from this ideal. The main reason for this failure is that we are studying people, and people (unlike radio waves or carbon atoms) are all individual in indefinitely many ways. Furthermore, our experiment must take place in a particular place and time, and how each individual responds to that experimental situation may also be influenced by indefinitely many external variables. You only have to discuss a film with a group of people to realise that the way people perceive and understand and appreciate the world varies enormously. Although there is a branch of psychology specifically devoted to understanding these individual differences, in the main field of experimental psychology with which we are concerned here we are hoping to draw general laws and theories that will be true of everyone. When we claim that common words are easier to recall than uncommon ones, this is a claim about a general tendency that we expect everyone to show. To find evidence for it, however, we have to be prepared to allow that, on some occasions, some individuals are not going to support the hypothesis. It may be that the particular uncommon words on the list have some special interest or meaning for one individual and end up being better recalled. Most psychological findings are therefore expressed as statistical or group results—that *on average* people will respond to our experimental manipulation in a particular way.

The between-subjects experiment

We are now ready to describe the construction of a *between-subjects* experiment. This is an experiment in which different groups of individuals perform under different conditions, and the performance of each group is then compared (usually by comparing the group average or mean) to see whether the condition a person was in had some effect on the dependent variable. As I described before, a common use of between-subjects designs is to compare a group in an experimental condition with a group in a control condition. (A condition is a particular set of procedures and materials to which a participant in the experiment is submitted.) We want to arrange that the two conditions are identical in all respects except for the critical factor that we are testing—the value of the independent variable. Where some other factor also differs systematically between the conditions, then we call this a *confounding variable* or factor, and it undermines our ability to interpret the results of the experiment. In effect we cannot tell which of the two variables was responsible for any observed difference in the dependent variable. It may even be the case that the two variables were working in opposite directions and cancelling each other out, leading to a null result. It is therefore critically important to avoid confounding variables in your design.

In an ideal experiment, we would want to keep everything else that might affect the result constant between our two groups. Clearly this is impossible, given what we have just said about the irrepressible individuality of human participants. In the face of this variability, we have three possible choices to avoid the dangers of confounding variables (assuming that the design involves two groups of participants—see Chapter 3 for within-subject designs).

The first option is *randomisation*. Suppose you decide to have 10 subjects in each of your groups, which we will call groups A and B. Then you should prepare 20 index cards, and write an A on 10 of them and a B on the other 10. Shuffle the pack. As each participant is recruited to the experiment, the experimenter draws a card out of the pack at random, and allocates the participant to one condition or the other on this basis. The logic of this procedure is plain. If the participants differ in relevant respects (for example one has an excellent memory which she intends to show off, another is only doing the experiment for the money and intends to put a minimum of effort into learning the material, etc.) then by randomly allocating them to groups, all such possible confounding variables will be randomly distributed between the conditions. By using a statistical test, you can then put an actual value on the probability that the random assignment produced any observed difference between the groups. If the experimenter takes the additional step of *replicating* the experiment (which is after all only sensible if the result is to be shown to be robust), then the chances of a result being caused accidentally by uneven distribution of the participants between groups can be reduced to a very low level. The process of randomisation is central to performing experiments. However, while it does ensure no systematic bias between the groups, it can leave considerable variability within each group, which can cause problems. The second and third options provide ways of reducing this level of "noise".

The second option is to use *balanced groups*. In the situation where there is a very obvious and easily measured factor that is known to have a major effect on the dependent variable, then it makes more sense to arrange for each group to have the same mean and spread on that factor. A good example is the case of cognitive development where children's ages are known to have a strong effect on their ability to do any kind of cognitive task. If the population sampled has a range of ages, then rather than use random allocation regardless of age, and try to observe the effect of the independent variable through the noise produced by variability in age, a researcher may choose to pair up children of the same age, and then allocate one of each pair to each condition at random. In this situation, the statistical test used would take account of the pairing of children, by using a "related" test as if the design were a within-subject design (a design in which the same participant's performance is compared across conditions of the experiment). This kind of design compares each person with his/her "pair" in the other group, and so removes the problem of a potentially confounding variable, and at the same time removes individual variation within the group that could be attributed to age, making the statistical test more sensitive to group differences. The use of within-subject designs is explained in Chapter 3.

Finally, the third option is to obtain some "baseline" measure of performance for all participants, perhaps in a preliminary pre-test. This can be used to reduce the impact of individual differences on the experiment, and so greatly improve the power of the design. For example in reaction time experiments it is very noticeable that some people might take 3 seconds to make a decision that others can make in 700 milliseconds. If the experiment starts with a "warm-up" session, doing some simple reaction time task, then the average time from this task can be used as a baseline against which to measure the performance in the experiment proper. You can either simply subtract each participant's baseline time from the other times, before calculating the group mean and variance. Alternatively a more sophisticated approach is to use the statistical technique of analysis of covariance to adjust the individual scores for differences in baseline response times.

Why use a between-subjects design?

Compared with the within-subject design described in Chapter 3, it might appear that between-subjects experiments are an inefficient way of doing research. Given that recruiting participants is one of the most effortful parts of psychological research, one can be forgiven for wanting to make the most of each participant by measuring each one in more than one condition of the experiment. There are four main situations where between-subjects designs are required. One is where the independent variable is a "quasi-experimental" variable. A quasi-experimental variable is one that we cannot manipulate ourselves, but which we use as a basis for group selection. Examples are sex, age, and social class. We cannot ask participants to change their sex, age, or social class in order to test them under more than one condition of the experiment. These variables are almost always treated as between-subjects variables (except in the case of longitudinal studies where age may be taken as a within-subject factor.) The second situation is where there would be a carry-over effect from one test to the next. Suppose for example that the dependent variable is a test of reasoning ability. If a within-subjects design were used then it is very likely that participants might show learning, or "positive transfer" from the first task to the second. Alternatively if the dependent variable involved learning to categorise a set of figures into two classes, then having to learn a new categorisation rule might be negatively affected by the previous learning (negative transfer). More obviously if the experiment involves introducing an unexpected test (for example an incidental memory test for a set of words that have been rated in different ways), once the first test has been given, participants will no longer be naive as to the purpose of the experiment, and will not treat subsequent conditions in the same way. The third situation where between-subjects designs are preferred is where the length of the experiment would be such as to make unreasonable demands on the participant. Remember that many psychology experiments are quite tedious to participate in, and take care of your participants. You will get better results from two people each doing a task for 35 minutes, than from one individual who has to work at it for over an hour. You will also find it easier to recruit people to do the experiment if it is not too demanding of time and patience.

Finally, a between-subjects design is useful where there is a danger of running into so-called "range effects". Suppose you are interested in what affects people's ability to remember a set of faces that they are shown for a brief period. You want to manipulate whether the faces are well known (celebrity faces), as opposed to unknown, and see how the rate of forgetting changes as a function of whether the faces were originally presented full-face or in profile. If all the faces were presented together, then there is a risk that either the well known faces will be so well remembered that performance is near perfect for all participants (a *ceiling effect*), or, if the task is made harder to bring performance on the well known faces down, then the unfamiliar faces will hardly be remembered at all (a *floor effect*). Ceiling and floor effects are known as range effects, and they cause serious problems for experimental results. If all participants are getting near 100% or near

0% correct, then there will be no way to detect the effect of the full-face vs profile manipulation. The solution to this problem is to have different subject groups trying to remember the well known and the unfamiliar faces. You can then deliberately make the task harder for the first group and easier for the second, in order to get a level of memory performance that will be sensitive to the independent variable you are interested in.

SUMMARY

- In a controlled between-subjects experiment the experimental and control conditions need to be as similar as possible in all other aspects except the value of the independent variable.
- To reduce the effect of individual differences in a between-subjects design there are three options:
  (a) randomisation ensures no systematic bias between groups but leaves the possibility of large variability within each group;
  (b) where there is an obvious variable that will affect the results, balancing of participants in pairs between groups ensures that it will not affect the outcome;
  (c) where there are likely to be large overall individual differences in performance, the use of a baseline measure may be helpful.
- Between-subjects designs are recommended where:
  (a) a quasi-experimental factor like age or sex is involved;
  (b) there would be carry-over effects from one condition to the next;
  (c) running a participant in all conditions would place unreasonable demands on their time and patience;
  (d) there is a danger of floor or ceiling effects if both conditions are run at the same time.

Getting a result

As most psychology students know from an early stage in their course, psychology experiments usually end with a statistical test. The purpose of this test in experimental between-subjects designs is very simple. It is to decide whether the observed difference in the performance of the two groups as measured by the dependent variable is large enough (and in the right direction) to give us sufficient reason to suppose that the experimental manipulation has had its predicted effect. Statistical tests derive a test statistic (for example Mann Whitney's U, or Student's t) which compares the size of the observed difference between the groups with the difference that you would expect to occur as a result of the random allocation of participants to groups, assuming that the groups were treated identically. By calculating how often the statistic should reach a certain level assuming that the independent variable has had no effect at all (known as the *null hypothesis*), the test tells us the likelihood that the results were obtained simply as a fluke of the groups being imbalanced. (In fact the test lumps together the influence of individual difference variables, random factors, and any other random error in measurement and calls this the *error variance*.) If the probability that the observed difference would occur by chance is less than some criterion (usually 0.05) then psychologists feel justified in concluding that the independent variable does influence the dependent variable. Most reports in journals however look for stronger evidence than a single result with a 5% significance level—editors like to be thoroughly convinced that a result is not a fluke before allocating precious journal space to it.

Students are often confused about how to interpret their results when the significance test shows a significance level that is just above 5%. What a significance level of between 5% and 10% is showing us is that there is *weak* evidence for rejecting the null hypothesis. In effect we are in a state of uncertainty where we don't feel confident enough to reject the null hypothesis, but at the same time it seems unsatisfactory to simply retain the null hypothesis without any further comment. In this situation, it is common for authors to report the result as a "marginally non-significant" effect. Another phrase often used for such effects is "non-significant trends". The best advice is to draw attention to any statistical tests in the range of 5–10% significance in your results section. In your discussion of the experiment however be careful not to make any claims that such a result is statistically reliable—it is not. At best you can discuss your data as providing some indication that a more powerful experiment might show the effect to be reliable. (For a discussion of the power of experiments see the next section.)

The power of experiments

In designing your experiment, you are naturally concerned to maximise your chances of "getting a result", or being able to reject the null hypothesis. In doing so, what you are trying to do in technical terms is to maximise the *power* of your experiment. The power of an experiment is the likelihood (number of times out of 100) that the experiment will generate a significant test statistic, assuming that there is a real effect of the independent variable on the dependent

What to do when your results are significant or insignificant

Interpreting the result of a statistical test requires a particular logic, which goes back to the philosophical nature of induction and the scientific method. When a test comes out with a result that passes our significance criterion (e.g. 0.05), then we may conclude that it is unlikely that the null hypothesis is true. Hence we accept the experimental hypothesis (that the independent variable is influencing the dependent variable)—but you should not claim to have proved it beyond doubt. There can always be fluke results, so you should temper your claims to have found the truth, and merely argue that the experiment provides evidence that supports the predictions of the theory (or contradicts the predictions of some other theory).

When a statistical test shows no significant result, you should be even more cautious about your conclusions. It may be very tempting to claim "there was no significant difference between the experimental and control groups, so the independent variable has been proved to have no effect on the dependent variable", but this would be wrong. The reason is that there may be many other causes of the lack of significance in your experiment. Logically, the null hypothesis being true is only one of the possible causes of a lack of significance. It could equally be that:

- you didn't manipulate the independent variable sufficiently;
- you didn't measure the dependent variable successfully;
- you didn't have enough participants for the effect to be detected in your experiment.

This can lead to a rather frustrating situation, where it is actually very hard to prove the non-existence of an effect (it is the same logical task as trying to prove there are no black swans—an exhaustive search of all swans is necessary). Psychologists do, from time to time, tackle this problem, but it requires a great deal more time and effort than providing evidence for the *existence* of an effect. It requires running the experiment in many different ways, giving the phenomenon every possible chance of appearing, and then using a very powerful experiment with many participants to show that if there is any effect it must be smaller than a certain size. (A recent case in the science literature was the claim by two physicists to have created conditions for nuclear fusion in a test-tube at room temperature. It took many months of research effort in a range of laboratories to come to the conclusion that the effect was not replicable.) Students are well advised to stick to looking for positive results in their research projects.

variable of a certain size. Power depends on a number of aspects of your design:

(a) The size of the effect. The bigger the effect that the independent variable has, then the more powerful your experiment will be. That is to say that big effects produce significant results more often than small effects. How can you influence the size of the effect? Clearly you cannot do much about the laws of nature; some variables have large effects and others small. However you can bear the effect size in mind when setting up your independent variable. If, for example, you are studying effects of word frequency on reading time (the difference between common words like "apple" and uncommon words like "vertigo"), then make the difference in frequency between high and low frequency words as large as possible. If you are studying the effect of illumination on mood, then make sure your bright room is truly bright, and your dim room truly dim. If there is going to be an effect, then going for a large manipulation of the independent variable is a good plan for a first experiment. If the effect fails to appear, then chances are that it is relatively small anyway, and so may not have much theoretical interest.

(b) The size of the sample.   The law of large numbers in statistics entails that if you keep on allocating participants to two groups at random, then in the long run the mean for each group on *all* variables will converge on the same value. That is to say that the accuracy with which you can measure the true difference between the groups caused by the independent variable becomes greater and greater the larger the number of people in each group. The power of your experiment thus increases with the size of your sample. Unfortunately, the relationship is one of "diminishing returns", as the power increases as the square root of the number of people sampled. So to double the power you would need to quadruple the sample size. You should however be careful not to launch into an experiment without a clear idea of how many participants you will need to recruit. For obvious reasons it is not good practice to continue recruiting participants until your result is significant and then to stop!

(c) The variability within each group.   The experiment is trying to discriminate the effect of the independent variable against a background of variability in scores resulting from all the other variables that have been controlled through the process of random allocation to groups. The technical term for this background variability is "error variance". Clearly the lower this background level of noise is, then the more powerful the experiment will be at detecting the influence of the independent variable. There are ways of reducing the unwanted subject variability. One, discussed previously, is to balance groups for certain major variables which are known to have a major effect. A second way to reduce the error variance is to use a homogeneous group of participants. One of the reasons that many cognitive psychologists have used student populations for their experiments is that individual variation in levels of literacy, computer familiarity, motivation and educational background is much less within such a group than it would be for the population taken as a whole. Using a homogeneous subpopulation will therefore have a positive effect on the power of your experiment, but at a certain cost. The down-side of using only one group of people is that your results cannot be generalised beyond this group. What is true for undergraduate students may or may not be true for the remainder of the population. From your study you just cannot say either way. Of course psychologists do commonly claim greater generality for their results, but this is usually on the basis of an additional argument that the phenomena being studied (for example the range of common cognitive functions) are biologically determined and so likely to work in the same way across the whole human race. Working with a homogeneous group therefore has distinct advantages, but you should be ready to qualify your results appropriately, and suggest that the results need replicating on other groups to investigate whether they still hold true.

(d) The significance level.   As power concerns the likelihood of the results achieving a particular significance level, it follows logically that if you set a lenient significance level you will achieve greater power. However this will be at the cost of producing a less convincing result. Most researchers in psychology stick to a 5% significance criterion, although it is often noted that there may be good reasons for varying this criterion depending on the utility of the result. If you wish to establish that there is a possible effect that is worthy of further investigation, then a 10% level might be a logical one to use, particularly if the costs of running the experiment will be high. In fact pilot experiments are very commonly used in psychology research to establish the smooth working of the procedures and to get a rough estimate of likely sample sizes needed. Alternatively if you wish to prove to the world that you can read people's thoughts you had better be prepared to achieve a very rigorous significance level, and to replicate the effect in a variety of situations.

(e) The sensitivity of your dependent measure.   Although not part of the formal definition of statistical power, the likelihood of a successful result can also be greatly reduced if you choose an inappropriate dependent measure. Ideally your dependent measure should be as sensitive as possible. For example, response times measured in milliseconds are a very sensitive measure, because the possible range is divided into a large number of different intervals. However success or failure on a reasoning task is a very insensitive measure, because each subject receives a score of simply 1 (pass) or 0 (fail). Try to devise a dependent measure that will give you at least 10 possible values on the measurement scale—for example by using 10 quick reasoning tasks rather than one long one—so that the effect of the independent variable has a chance to show up. Another major factor affecting sensitivity is the problem of floor and ceiling effects. Suppose that you run a memory experiment in which people have to recall a list of 10 words, and when you examine the results 90% of the subjects in the two groups have got a perfect 10 out of 10 correct. We described this before as a ceiling effect, because performance has hit the top of the scale. The converse problem occurs where a large proportion of subjects are recalling just one or no items—performance is at the floor level. Floor and ceiling effects can severely restrict the sensitivity of your dependent variable. You cannot reasonably detect differences between the groups if they are both finding the task so easy (or so difficult). Judicious use of a pilot experiment on a few people is advisable where these effects may occur in order to check that performance is at the most sensitive middle portion of the scale. As well as memory tests, floor and ceiling effects may also occur in tests of reasoning and problem solving, if the tasks are too hard or too easy.

SUMMARY

- Statistical tests are almost always used with psychology experiments.
- They provide a measure of the likelihood that the difference in performance between the two groups was the result of random allocation of participants to groups.
- The probability of finding a significant result in your sample when there is actually an effect in the population is the statistical power of the experiment.
- Statistical power depends on:
  (a) effect size;
  (b) sample size;
  (c) within-group variability;
  (d) significance level.
- Experiments may also lack power if the dependent measure is insensitive.

Factorial designs

In the final section, we will look briefly at the design of experiments involving more than two groups of participants. In the first case, you may have an independent variable that can be fixed at a range of different levels. To take an example, you may be interested in how the level of illumination in a room affects exam performance. Now it is likely that if taken to extremes performance is going to decrease at both ends of the scale. People cannot see in the dark, nor can they function in a dazzling glare. In this case, what is needed is a sampling of different levels of illumination across a range of values. In terms of design, the same principles as previously discussed still hold. Participants should be allocated to conditions entirely at random, and sufficient numbers used in each group to permit a satisfactory power to be achieved. Choices of which levels of illumination to use should bear in mind that small differences in level are likely to generate small effects which may be hard to detect. Start with just three or four fairly large differences in level. This should give you a rough idea of where the performance is best, and could be followed up with more levels if needed to find the actual optimum level. Statistically, a rather different approach is required, as you are no longer comparing an experimental group with a control group.

In the second case, you may have a design in which you wish to manipulate more than one independent variable at the same time. In this case, the independent variables are often called "factors". It is common in psychology for experiments to employ mixed designs in which one or more of the factors are treated as within-subject manipulations (see next chapter), as otherwise the problems of needing large numbers of participants to achieve reasonable power are multiplied considerably. Although many students (perhaps fired up with their evident skill in experimental design) feel tempted to build large and elaborate designs, it is good practice to avoid running experiments with too many independent variables at once, at least at the start of a research project. The reasons for this advice are simple. First of all, the more factors that are included, the less powerful the design becomes without increasing the number of participants, or the number of measurements taken from each participant (and hence the length and complexity of the task). Second, and more importantly it is essential to know that your experimental procedures are working before attempting to develop more elaborate designs. In discussing the logic of experimentation earlier in this chapter, I pointed out that few scientists in practice spend all their efforts trying to falsify hypotheses. If your experiment fails, then it could be that your hypothesis was wrong, but it could equally be that any other step in the chain of reasoning and assumptions that took you from the theoretical proposition to the practical manipulation and measurements that you took could be false. Perhaps the independent variable didn't really reflect the theoretical variable that it was intended to, perhaps the dependent variable measured was insensitive to the underlying change in the individual that you intended to measure. In order to derive predictions from theories about concrete experimental situations it is always necessary to make assumptions. If the experiment fails it could be because of the falsehood of one of these assumptions.

The moral is that your first experiment should aim to establish a robust and strong effect which shows to the world that you have created or recreated a phenomenon in your lab that can be studied. Subsequent experiments can then be directed at looking at whether the "effect" changes in ways predicted (or not predicted) by theory when submitted to other independent variables. (We sometimes talk about achieving *experimental control* over a phenomenon when we find a variety of conditions with which we can make it appear and disappear at will.) Finally, if the cognitive process is sufficiently understood to permit a model of the process to be proposed, then the more subtle predictions of the model—for example about the way in which one independent variable may *interact* with another in modulating the effect—may be tested in multifactorial experiments.

SUMMARY

- Between-subjects designs may also be used with an independent variable with more than two conditions.
- Avoid having too many "levels" at once, as power is reduced.
- Factorial designs employ more than one independent variable at the same time.
- When designing a research project "start simple", and only introduce complex factorial designs when you have demonstrated robust effects with simpler designs.

Exercises (may best be done in groups of three or four students)

1. Plan a between-subjects design to investigate the way in which fatigue affects medical decision making. Pay careful attention to the problems of defining independent and dependent variables, and to maximising the power of your experiment.

2. Analyse the concept of "explanation". Think of as many different examples of the use of the concept as you can, and discuss what they have in common (if anything). How does the concept apply to theories in psychology?

3. Taking the example of fatigue and decision making (or any other example you choose), see how many different independent variables and different dependent variables you can devise which could be used to test the influence of the one upon the other.

References

Popper, K.R. (1972). *Objective knowledge*. Oxford: Oxford University Press.

Roethlisberger, F.J., & Dickson, W.J. (1964). *Management and the worker*. New York: John Wiley.

Within-subject designs 3

Elizabeth J. Hellier

Introduction

In the experiments that have been considered so far, different subjects are assigned to different groups, (either to experimental treatment groups or to a control group) and their scores are compared to look for evidence of an effect of the independent variable or variables. This kind of design is termed a *between-subjects design* because scores are compared between different subjects in different groups. Let us look at an example. If you wanted to investigate the extent to which glare affects performance on a computer-based reading task, you could use a between-subjects design. You would divide the subjects into two groups and measure some aspects of their performance (such as reading speed and text comprehension) under different conditions of glare. Group 1 might perform the task while there was glare on the screen, whereas Group 2 would perform the same task, but without glare on the screen. You could measure reading speed and text comprehension for the two groups and compare their scores on each measure (Table 3.1). Providing you had controlled the experiment adequately so that extraneous variables were not influencing subjects' reading speed or text comprehension scores, then you could infer that any differences between the scores for the two groups were caused by the presence or absence of glare on the screen.

In the example shown in Table 3.1, scores for Group 1 are worse on both reading speed (they are slower) and comprehension (they are less accurate) and so it appears that the presence of glare degrades these aspects of performance on a computer-based reading task. There is, however, an alternative explanation for this set of data. It is possible that the subjects in Group 2 may have been faster readers and/or have had better reading comprehension skills than the subjects in Group 1.

TABLE 3.1
Between-subjects
design to
investigate the
effect of glare on
performance of a
computer-
based task.

	Group 1 (s. 1–10) Glare	Group 2 (s. 11–20) No glare
Reading speed (sec.)	40	30
Text comprehension (% correct)	75	85

s. = subjects

If that were that case, then differences in scores between the two groups could have been a result of differences in the skills that subjects brought with them to the experiment, rather than the experimental manipulation itself. In between-subjects designs this possibility is avoided by *balancing* subjects in the different experimental conditions so that they have similar skill levels (see Chapter 2). Sometimes however, it can be difficult to balance subjects, and when that is the case, there is an alternative experimental design that might be more appropriate to use.

Instead of dividing the sample of subjects into two groups as in the example just given, you could just use one group of subjects and let them perform in both the glare and no glare conditions (Table 3.2). In fact, this is what Garcia and Wierwille did when they investigated the effects of glare on computer-based reading speed and text comprehension in 1985. They compared each subject's scores in the glare condition with the same subject's scores in the no glare condition. Here, the subjects are balanced in terms of their skills because the same subjects are performing in both conditions.

Experiments designed in this way are most commonly termed *within-subject designs*. The same subjects perform in all experimental conditions and a subject's score in one condition, and their score in the other conditions are compared. Comparisons are thus within the scores of the same subject. There are alternative terms for this type of experiment that highlight, and may help you to remember, different features of the design. The term *repeated measures design*, is used

	Group 1 (s. 1–20) Glare	Group 2 (s. 1–20) No glare
Reading speed (sec.)	40	30
Text comprehension (% correct)	75	85

s. = subjects

TABLE 3.2 Within-subject design to investigate the effect of glare on performance of a computer-based task.

because the subjects are measured repeatedly, they are measured in each different condition; while the term *between-conditions design* reflects the fact that the same subject's scores are compared between experimental conditions. Within-subject designs are also one of a class of *related designs*—the scores in different conditions are related in that they belong to the same subject.

Aims

In this chapter examples of common within-subject designs will be considered to help you get a better idea of what a within-subject design is. The strengths and limitations of this approach to experimentation will be reviewed, as will techniques for avoiding some of the limitations. This work will be drawn together to guide your selection of a between-subjects versus a within-subject design in different circumstances. Lastly, there are some exercises that will help you to consolidate what you have read about within-subject and between-subjects designs.

At the end of this chapter you should be able to:

- say what a within-subject design is;
- understand the strengths and weaknesses of within-subject designs;
- have the skill to select whether a between-subjects or a within-subject design is most appropriate to investigate different experimental questions.

SUMMARY

In a within-subject design:

- the same subjects perform in all of the experimental conditions;
- comparisons are made between one individual's scores in different conditions;
- comparisons are within the scores of the same subject.

Examples of common within-subject designs

In this section examples of common within-subject designs will be reviewed so that you can get a clearer idea of what they are and can see how they work in practice.

Psychophysical studies

Within-subject designs are frequently used when the independent variable has many levels. Many levels of the independent variable means many experimental conditions (different levels of the independent variable being tested in each experimental condition). This often means that it is not practical to use a between-subjects design because it would require many different groups of subjects, one to be tested in each experimental condition. Within-subject designs are often used for this reason in psychophysics, an area of psychology dedicated to equating changes in sensation (psycho) to actual physical changes in a stimulus (physics). For example, Stevens (1956) was interested in the relationship between the subjective experience of loudness and the physical intensity of a sound. By how much do you think you have to change the physical intensity of a sound in order to for it to be perceived as twice as loud ? For it to be perceived as half as loud? To address these questions, Stevens conducted experiments that required subjects to listen to sounds that varied in decibels (dB) and to judge how loud each stimulus appeared to be. In this way Stevens was able to relate changes in dB to changes in perceived loudness. In experiments such as these there is essentially one independent variable, the dB of the sound, and one dependent variable, subjects' perceptions of loudness. The independent variable, however, has many levels. Stevens presented his subjects with nine levels of the independent variable—sounds at nine different levels between 30 and 100dB (from a quiet whisper to a pneumatic drill). In a between-subjects design nine groups of subjects would be needed here, one group to judge each level of the independent variable, each sound. This is obviously unwieldy and so it is preferable to use one group of subjects to judge all of the sounds. If you do this, each subject is repeatedly measured, they judge the perceived loudness of the sound at 30 dB, at 40dB and so on, and judgements of the different stimuli are compared within the same subject.

Learning studies

In the previous example a within-subject design was used to investigate the effects of the independent variable as a matter of convenience. There are also occasions when a within-subject design is the only appropriate choice of design because the independent variable of interest has to be measured within the same subject. Consider as an example a learning experiment. Seligman and Maier (1967) exposed dogs to inescapable electric shocks over time and then found that when the same dogs were subsequently able to escape the electric shock by leaping over a barrier, they did not do so. They termed this phenomenon "learned helplessness": the dogs had learned, from repeated exposures to the shock, that it was unavoidable, and thus they stopped seeking escape behaviours. This phenomenon relies on an individual learning over time and can only be demonstrated if the same subjects are exposed to all the learning conditions, in a within-subject design.

Pre-test/Post-test designs

A special case of a within-subject design is the pre-test/post-test paradigm. In this paradigm subjects are measured on the dependent variable once, then they are exposed a single treatment, and then they are measured on the dependent variable again. Any change in their measurements on the dependent variable between the pre and post test is assumed to be as a result of the intervening treatment. This paradigm is crucially different from the learning paradigm just described because subjects only receive a single treatment or level of the independent variable, sandwiched between the pre and post tests. This simple paradigm is often used to investigate the effectiveness of programs and interventions in the "real world". If, for example, you wanted to measure the effectiveness of a "Don't Drink and Drive" campaign, you might measure the levels of self-reported drink driving in a given sample (pre test). You could then run an Anti Drink Drive campaign for several weeks (the treatment) before measuring levels of self-reported drink driving again in the same sample (post test).

Factorial within-subject designs

The previous examples have focused on within-subject designs that have looked at the effects of one independent variable (*single factor within-subject designs*). Within-subject designs can also be used to investigate the effects of two or more independent variables (*factorial within-subject designs*). When Garcia and Wierwille (1985) investigated the effects of glare on performance of a reading task they were also interested in whether the effects of glare were mediated by the difficulty of the reading material. Therefore their experiment investigated two independent variables, screen condition (glare and no glare) and subjective text difficulty (ranging from easy to difficult). The subjects had to perform the reading task at all levels of the independent variables, when there was glare and the text was easy, when there was glare and the text was difficult, when there was no glare and the text was easy, and when there was no glare and the text was difficult. Garcia and Wierwille found that the presence of glare increased the time taken to read subjectively easy texts but decreased the time taken to read subjectively difficult texts. You can see from this example that subjects performed at all levels of all the independent variables, they were repeatedly measured, and so this is a within-subject design.

SUMMARY

Examples have been chosen to give you a feel for the range of areas in which within-subject designs are used; you will soon be able to identify many more examples, just remember what you are looking for:

- designs where the same subjects are *repeatedly measured* on all levels of the independent variable(s);
- designs where scores are compared *within the same subject, between their judgements on different conditions*.

Advantages of within-subject designs

Once you do start looking for examples, you will see that many experiments in psychology are within-subject. In part, this is because some areas of investigation require the same subjects to receive all of the experimental conditions, such as learning experiments, or instances where the experimenter is interested in how subjects judge the relative differences between levels of the independent variable. In addition, within-subject designs are sometimes chosen because of the advantages that they have for the experimenter. These advantages are reviewed next.

Power

You have already been introduced to the notion of experimental power—the likelihood that your experiment will find a significant effect, when an effect exists. Chapter 2 described the circumstances under which the power of an experiment is increased, and included the observation that reducing variability within the subject group was an important means of increasing experimental power. As within-subject designs use the same subjects in all conditions, subject variability is minimised. This makes within-subject design an inherently powerful one that maximises your chances of "getting a result".

Subject as their own control

If you think back to the first example that we used, an experiment to investigate the effects of glare on performance, we said that to run the experiment between-subjects, subjects in the different groups would have to be matched or balanced for their reading and comprehension skills. In a within-subject design, there is no need to go to the trouble of balancing the subjects on selected attributes—they are already balanced because it is the same subjects that participate in the different conditions. An individual subject's scores in one condition are compared with their scores in other conditions and so the *subject is acting as his/her own control.*

Subject numbers

Within-subject designs require fewer subjects than between-subjects designs. Think again of the experiment to investigate the effects of glare; for a between-subjects design you needed two groups of subjects, one to be tested in each condition. If you wanted 10 scores from each condition then you would need 10 subjects in each condition, a total of 20 subjects. If you ran the experiment as a within-subject design however, to achieve the same 10 scores from each condition, you only need 10 subjects in total. This is because each subject provides you with 10 scores in condition 1 and

10 scores in condition 2, the same 20 scores, but provided by only 10 subjects. Think also of Stevens's (1956) experiment on perceived loudness; if he wanted 10 scores for each of the 9 sounds at different dB levels, a between-subjects design would mean that he would need to find 90 subjects, 10 subjects to judge the first sound, 10 to judge the second and so on to the ninth sound. Running this study within-subject, however, would necessitate the use of only 10 subjects, because each subject could provide nine judgements, one for each sound. In general, to get the same number of scores, you need far fewer subjects if the design is within-subject. This is an important advantage when the subjects you need are from a specific population that is difficult to get hold of, or when using a between-subjects design would require you to find more subjects than is practical.

Running time and costs

Within-subject designs mean that, after the subjects have performed in the first condition, the main procedural instructions do not need to be reiterated in detail before each subsequent condition. This is an important time saver if instructions are particularly lengthy or complex, or if subjects need detailed training before they can take part in a study.

So you can see that there are certainly pragmatic advantages to selecting a within-subject design for your experiments. As always in psychology there is another side to the argument, and before you rush off and conduct all your experiments within-subject, it is important that you understand that these designs have some important limitations. These limitations will affect the way in which you conduct your experiment in order to overcome them, and may even preclude the use of a within-subject design to investigate certain topics.

SUMMARY

Within-subject designs have many advantages:

- they are powerful;
- the subject is used as his/her own control;
- they require less subjects;
- they can reduce running time and costs.

Limitations of within-subject designs

Using the same subjects in all experimental conditions gives rise to certain phenomena that, if uncontrolled, threaten the internal validity of your experiment. These phenomena will be reviewed here and techniques for controlling them will be introduced in the next section.

Order effects

Order effects arise from the fact that if the same subjects do all of the conditions in an experiment then they must necessarily complete them in a particular sequence or order. Sometimes the order in which they complete the conditions influences their scores and when that happens, the treatment is no longer the only thing influencing their scores—the order of the conditions is also doing so. Thus the experimental effect and the order effects are confounded. There are many variations in the way that order effects are categorised and discussed (see for example, Davis 1995; Elmes, Kantowitz, & Roediger 1995; or Harris 1986). Here order effects have been categorised as either *practice effects* or *carryover effects*. Each of these terms is explained next.

Practice effects.   Practice effects arise when a subject's scores in a second or subsequent experimental condition are affected by the fact that they have performed the experiment before—i.e. they have had practice. Consider our example of the effects of glare on performance of a computer-based reading task. Subjects had to perform a reading task in the glare condition and also to perform a reading task again in the no glare condition. If subjects were given the same passage to read in both conditions, then you might expect their reading speed and comprehension to improve in the second condition regardless of the effect of glare, but because they had read the passage before. When subjects' performance improves in a second or subsequent condition as a result of performing in the experiment before then this is referred to as a *positive practice effect*. Positive practice effects may arise not only because subjects have performed the actual experimental task before, but also because they are less anxious about the experimental setting or measures in the second condition.

Alternatively, subjects in the glare experiment might have been asked to read an extract of *David Copperfield* from the screen for one hour in the glare condition, and then to continue reading from the text for another hour in the no glare condition. In these circumstances you might expect their scores to get worse in the second condition, not as an effect of glare, but as a result of fatigue or boredom. When subjects' performance gets worse in a second or subsequent experimental condition, they are exhibiting *negative practice effects*. Such effects are usually the result of boredom, fatigue, or loss of motivation for the task (which can be caused by a feeling that they have previously performed very well or very badly).

Carryover effects. Practice effects arise in the second and subsequent conditions of an experiment just because the subject has performed in the experiment before. Carryover effects are a particular type of order effect that arise because a particular condition has been performed before another one and the effects of this condition carry over to influence performance in subsequent conditions. As Davis (1995) points out, these effects can arise from several possible sources.

Carryover effects might be caused by skills that a subject develops or instructions that a subject receives in one condition that affect their performance on the following conditions. For example, if you were investigating whether using an analogy can help people solve problems, you might have two conditions, an analogy and a no analogy condition. It would be easy for subjects who had been in the no analogy condition first to be instructed to perform a problem-solving task with an analogy in the second condition. If the subjects had been in the analogy condition first, however, then it would be very difficult for them not to use that analogy to help them solve the problem in the no analogy condition. The effects of instructions in the analogy condition would carry over to influence subjects' performance in the next condition.

Carryover effects can also be caused by subjects interpreting the purpose of the experiment in one condition and this interpretation influencing their performance in the next condition. In the example just given, subjects are likely to notice that the only difference between the two conditions is the presence or absence of an analogy. They may then guess your hypothesis and change their behaviour to either "help" you support your hypothesis or to refute it. (Many subjects in psychology experiments are, after all, budding psychologists themselves.) Either way, they cease to be naive subjects.

Lastly, carryover effects can be caused by one level of the independent variable still explicitly having an influence over the subject when they come to be tested on the next level. This might be the case if you were investigating the influence of marijuana on memory. Subjects who had to memorise a passage in a no marijuana condition could go on to memorise a passage in the marijuana condition. If you ran the conditions the other way round, however, then subjects who had already had marijuana would still have it in their system and this would influence their performance in the no marijuana condition. It is usually the case that carryover effects are present because one particular condition has been performed before another, and they would not be present if the conditions were performed in the reverse order. The possible exception to this are the carryover effects caused by subjects losing their naivety as the experiment progresses, but even then, it is often the case that an experiment is more transparent to a subject if the conditions are presented in one order rather than another.

Subject dropout

Because within-subject designs necessitate testing the same subjects under all levels of the independent variable(s) you need the subjects to be present for the whole of your experiment. If the experimental testing is short and can be conducted in one sitting, this is rarely a problem. If, however, your experimental procedures are lengthy and/or you need subjects to return for repeat testing on separate occasions, you may find that it is difficult to get enough subjects who are available on the occasions that you need them. Alternatively, you may find that some subjects drop out of the study because they do not return for repeat testing when you asked them to. As you need subjects to have performed in all of the experimental conditions, you can therefore be left with data from fewer subjects than you wanted.

Designing equivalent materials

When the glare experiment was considered previously, you might have wondered whether subjects were expected to read a passage of text in one condition, and then to read the same passage again in the second condition. Well, they were not. This is because reading the same passage of text in both conditions would incur practice effects leading to improvement in the second condition regardless of whether or not glare was present. In instances like this, when you cannot just repeat stimulus materials between conditions because of practice effects, you need to provide different materials for each condition. However, it is important that the materials do not differ too much between conditions. If they do, then it might be differences in the materials that cause differences in performance rather than the independent variable. To create stimulus materials for the same subjects to work on in different conditions that are not identical but not too different either, you need to *match materials* between conditions. For a reading task this is easy. Different passages can be constructed that are the same length, have the same syntactic complexity, the same word frequency and length, and that address the same type of subject matter. For other experimental scenarios however it can be more difficult to construct equivalent stimulus materials and this can limit the use of within-subject designs in some circumstances.

The limitations that have been considered are important and, if left unchecked, can seriously threaten the internal validity of your experiment. This does not mean that you need to give up on within-subject designs. Happily there are ways of administering within-subject designs that can counteract the effects of some of these limitations. These procedures will be reviewed next.

SUMMARY

Within-subject designs have some important limitations:

- order effects such as practice effects or carryover effects;
- the problems of subject dropout;
- the need to design matched experimental materials to use in different conditions.

Overcoming the limitations of within-subject designs

The problems of subject dropout and of designing equivalent materials in within-subject designs cannot really be avoided. If equivalent materials are going to be impossible to create or if subject availability is likely to be a big problem then you may need to consider a between-subjects design. Criteria for helping you make that choice will be covered in more detail in the next section. Specific carryover effects such as the effects of experimental doses of alcohol or drugs can be avoided by leaving enough elapsed time between experimental conditions (but watch for subject dropout when you do this). The major limitation of within-subject designs, order effects, can be addressed through experimental procedures. These procedures are outlined in detail by Shaughnessy and Zechmeister (1985) and are reviewed here.

Order effects arise when the order in which subjects do conditions in an experiment influences their performance. In order to understand how to avoid such effects, consider as an example the glare experiment with subjects doing the conditions in the order, glare followed by no glare. You might find that subjects had comprehension scores of 20 in the glare condition and 40 in the no glare condition. From what you know about practice effects, this could be for one of two reasons. It could be because the absence of glare made the task easier for the subjects in the no glare condition *or* because they had practice of the task in the glare condition previously and this practice had improved their performance. How do you overcome this confounding of the experimental effect and the practice effect? You need to balance any improvement in scores as a result of practice between the experimental conditions so each condition is affected equally by practice. This is achieved by requiring subjects to complete the experimental conditions in different orders. One way you might go about this is to have half of the subjects perform the experiment in the order glare followed by no glare, and the other half of the subjects perform the experiment in the order no glare followed by glare. If you do this, then any increment in subjects' scores as a result of practice will not just distort the scores for the no glare condition, but will be added to scores in both conditions equally. This is because half of the subjects will have had any practice effect added to their scores in the glare condition (they did this second) and the other half of the subjects will have had any practice effects added to their scores in the no glare condition (they did this second). In this way, any distortion to scores as a result of practice is balanced equally between the two conditions. Differences that remain in scores should be a result of the experimental treatment.

Counterbalancing

The procedure just demonstrated is called *counterbalancing*. The order in which different subjects perform experimental conditions is varied so that order effects are balanced between conditions and, rather than just distorting scores in one condition, they distort scores in all conditions by an equal amount and thus cancel each other out. One way of varying the order of conditions between subjects is to use a procedure called *complete counterbalancing*.

Complete counterbalancing.   With complete counterbalancing, all possible orders of experimental conditions are presented an equal number of times. Each condition precedes and follows each other condition, in each ordinal position (1st, 2nd, 3rd etc.), an equal number of times. An equal number of subjects perform the conditions in each of the orders. For the glare experiment with two conditions this would mean that half the subjects performed conditions in the order glare followed by no glare, while the other half of the subjects performed the condition in the order no glare followed by glare. This was the example used earlier. Complete counterbalancing is simple to achieve when there are only two experimental conditions. However, because all possible orders of conditions must be presented, and because an equal number of subjects must perform the conditions in each different order, complete counterbalancing becomes unwieldy when there are more than about four experimental conditions. Six experimental conditions means that there are 720 possible orders that the conditions could be presented in (that is $6 \times 5 \times 4 \times 3 \times 2 \times 1$ orders). To completely counterbalance such an experiment you would need at least one subject to perform the conditions in each order (because you need an equal number of subjects to perform in each condition); that is, 720 subjects. In order to get around this requirement for so many subjects, incomplete counterbalancing procedures also exist that can be used to balance order effects when you have more than three or four experimental conditions.

Incomplete counterbalancing. With incomplete counterbalancing, only some of all the possible orders of experimental conditions are used to balance out order effects. One of the most common procedures for achieving incomplete counterbalancing is to use a *balanced Latin Square Design*. In a balanced Latin Square Design, each condition is presented equally often in each ordinal position (1st, 2nd, 3rd, etc.) and each condition precedes and follows each other one (but this does not happen equally often in each ordinal position). An example of a balanced Latin Square Design for a four-condition experiment with 20 subjects is presented in Table 3.3. There are four different orders of conditions for the experiment which are read across the rows. An equal number of subjects is needed to perform the experiment in each of the four orders. As you can see from this table, each condition is presented in each ordinal position (for example, condition A is presented 1st, 2nd, 3rd, and 4th), and each condition precedes and follows each other one (for example, condition A precedes and follows each of conditions B, C, and D). Alternatively, but less commonly, you could use a *block randomised Latin Square Design* whereby the order of the conditions in each row is determined randomly. Detailed instructions of how to create your own Latin Square Designs are presented by Elmes et al. (1995).

TABLE 3.3
A balanced Latin
Square Design
for an experiment
with four
conditions.

	Conditions
Order 1 (s. 1–5)	A B D C
Order 2 (s. 6–10)	B C A D
Order 3 (s. 11–15)	C D B A
Order 4 (s. 16–20)	D A C B

s. = subjects

An alternative method of achieving incomplete counterbalancing is to use a procedure called *randomisation and rotation*. With this method, you begin with a random order of conditions and then for each subsequent order you rotate the conditions once to the left until you are back at the starting position. With this procedure each condition appears in each ordinal position equally often, but does not precede and follow each other one equally often. An example of randomisation and rotation for a four-condition experiment is shown in Table 3.4.

	Conditions
Order 1 (s. 1–5)	B C A D
Order 2 (s. 6–10)	C A D B
Order 3 (s. 11–15)	A D B C
Order 4 (s. 16–20)	D B C A

s. = subjects

TABLE 3.4
Randomisation
and rotation for
an experiment
with four
conditions.

Randomisation

An alternative procedure for minimising order effects when you have a lot of experimental conditions is *randomisation*. Randomisation means that the order in which each subject does the experimental conditions is randomly determined. The random orders for each subject can easily be achieved on a computer or by pulling the conditions out of a hat. With this method you would expect order effects to be approximately balanced between conditions because for each subject, each condition has an equal chance of appearing in each ordinal position.

The counterbalancing and randomisation procedures reviewed here can also be used to help you assign subjects to different conditions in between-subjects designs and to decide the order in which subjects are tested on one of several dependent variables. You should be aware that when these procedures are used, as in the examples given, to counteract the effects of order between subjects, they result in what are called *incomplete within-subject designs*. This is because order effects are balanced out over the whole group of subjects, not for each individual subject. In *complete within-subject designs*, order effects are balanced out for each individual by requiring each subject to perform the experimental conditions several times in different orders. Procedures for deciding the different orders of conditions for individual subjects in complete within-subject designs are outlined in detail in Shaughnessy and Zechmeister (1985). The procedures outlined here are the ones that you are most likely to use to counteract the possibility of order effects, so overcoming the most important limitation of within-subject designs. There are some circumstances when these procedures are not sufficient to counteract order effects, and in these circumstances the use of a within-subject design is ill-advised. Such circumstances will be covered in the next section when some rules of thumb to help you choose between a within-subject and a between-subjects design will be considered.

SUMMARY

- The major limitation of within-subject designs is order effects.
- These can be overcome by using counterbalancing procedures (complete/incomplete) or randomisation.
- These procedures equalise order effects between experimental conditions so that they cancel each other out.

Choosing a within-subject or a between-subjects design

Choosing a within-subject design

On a practical level, within-subject designs require you to find fewer subjects and can be faster to run. Beyond that, within-subject designs are the only appropriate choice of design in some circumstances, such as when you want to investigate changes in one group of individuals over time, as in the case of learning, transfer, or memory studies. Conversely, sometimes aspects of your enquiry will preclude the use of a within-subject design. Some of the things to look out for when you are considering a potential experiment that may mean you should use a between-subjects design are listed next.

Choosing a between-subjects design

Asymmetrical order effects. The procedures that were outlined to counteract order effects in within-subject experiments assume that any order effects are symmetrical—that is, they are of the same direction and magnitude whichever order the conditions are presented in. This is not always the case. *Asymmetrical order effects* occur when an order effect is different when conditions are presented in one order as compared to when they are presented in another order. The carryover effects reviewed earlier are essentially asymmetrical order effects. As an example, if you were investigating the effects of noise on subjects' ability to do a problem-solving task, you might have two conditions, noise and no noise. If subjects completed the experiment in the order noise followed by no noise then there may be a practice effect arising from the fact that subjects had done a similar problem-solving task in the first condition. If, however, they completed the experiment in the reverse order, no noise followed by noise, then that practice effect may be much larger. This could be because subjects were able to concentrate more on the problem-solving task when they had the no noise condition first than when they had the noise condition first. This extra concentration in the first condition may lead to greater familiarity with the task and so to more of a practice effect. In such circumstances, order effects vary in size depending on the order in which the subject does the conditions, they are asymmetrical. When order effects are likely to be asymmetrical, between-subjects designs should be employed because the procedures outlined previously to control for order effects in within-subject designs can only control for symmetrical, not asymmetrical, order effects.

Range effects.   Chapter 2 introduced range effects and described how between-subjects designs were a useful way of minimising their influence. When there is a potential for range effects in your experiment, which means that presenting both conditions together is likely to result in floor or ceiling effects, then within-subject designs should be avoided.

Area of investigation.   It was noted earlier that there were some areas of investigation that necessitate the used of a within-subject design. Conversely, there are other areas of investigation that preclude the use of a within-subject design. First, if subject variables such as gender, age, or nature of cognitive impairment are the independent variables of interest then you cannot use a within-subject design. (One individual could only ever be in one condition for such variables, they could not be run in both an "old" and "young" condition for example.) Second, within-subject designs cannot be used if the treatment has very lasting or permanent effects on the subject. For example, if you were comparing the effectiveness of different styles of machine training for operators in the workplace, a subject could not be trained to use the machine in one way and then unlearn it to be trained another way. The effects of the independent variable of training are too permanent for a within-subject design to be of use. Third, if your area of investigation necessitates that subjects are naive in all experimental conditions, you cannot use a within-subject design. Imagine a deception experiment in which subjects received a surprise at the end of each condition that revealed to them the nature of the deception. The same subjects could not repeat the experiment in a second condition because they would already know the deception that was involved.

SUMMARY

In this section some factors that can be used to guide your choice of a within-subject or a between-subjects design have been reviewed. A useful rule of thumb might be to choose a within-subject design if:

- it is not precluded by the likelihood of asymmetrical order effects or range effects;
- it is not precluded by the subject of your inquiry.

In addition, incidental learning studies with several conditions preclude the use of within-subject designs. You might, for example, be trying to measure how much flight safety information subjects can remember after different styles of in-flight safety briefing. You would not be able to use the same subjects in different conditions because their incidental learning on one condition would carry over to influence their learning on another. These examples demonstrate that in some circumstances and for some areas of investigation a within-subject design is not an appropriate choice.

Exercises

The following exercises will help you to consolidate what you have read about within-subject and between-subjects designs. Write a brief paragraph (c.500 words) to answer each question.

1. What are the principal advantages of within-subject designs?
2. Think of three topics that you could not investigate using a within-subject design. Say why a within-subject design would not be suitable.
3. Outline the techniques for overcoming order effects in within-subject designs.

4. Redesign the Garcia and Wierwille (1985) study as a between-subjects experiment. What are the strengths and weaknesses of a between-subjects design for this investigation? Note how the strengths and weaknesses change when the study is within-subject. You can perform this exercise for many experiments that you come across in psychology. Doing so will help you to get a feel for the pros and cons of within-subject versus between-subjects designs in different situations.

References

Davis, A. (1995). The experimental methods in psychology. In G. Breakwell, S. Hammond, & C. Fife Shaw (Eds.), *Research methods in psychology* (pp. 50–68). London: Sage.

Elmes, D., Kantowitz, B., & Roediger, H. (1995). *Research methods in psychology.* (5th Edn.). St. Paul, MN: West Publishing Company.

Garcia, K., & Wierwille, W. (1985). Effect of glare on performance of a VDT reading-comprehension task. *Human Factors, 27*(2), 163–173.

Harris, P. (1986). *Designing and reporting experiments.* Milton Keynes, UK: Open University Press.

Seligman, M., & Maier, S. (1967). Failure to escape traumatic shock. *Journal of Experimental Psychology, 74,* 1–9.

Shaughnessy, J., & Zechmeister, E. (1985). *Research methods in psychology*. New York: Alfred A. Knopf.

Stevens, S., (1956). The direct estimation of sensory magnitudes—loudness. *American Journal of Psychology, LXXIX* No.1, 1–27.

Experimental versus correlational methods 4

Peter Ayton

This chapter contrasts the two main research formats used to collect data in psychology, the experimental and the correlational study. As we shall see, each of these two research formats has advantages and disadvantages—particularly in terms of the kinds of inferences that can be made from the data collected.

Aims

The aim of this chapter is to instil in the reader an understanding of the correlational approach to the study of behaviour—its merits as well as its limitations. The correlational approach in psychology is crucial for certain types of investigation. There are however important—but often overlooked—limitations to the approach. After reading this chapter the reader should appreciate how they might benefit from the appropriate application of correlational research designs.

The simple experiment: Active observation

Experiments are designed in order to explore the causality of measurable phenomena. Conducting an experiment means making some action and measuring the effect of that action. As we have seen (Chapters 2 and 3) an experimenter will manipulate an independent variable and look for changes in a dependent variable. The experimenter attempts to hold all other variables constant because otherwise these might be responsible for any observed variation in the dependent variable. For example if we were interested in the effects of noise on students' exam performance we might put some students into a noisy room and some into a quiet room and compare their exam results. However, if the noisy room was also much hotter than the quiet room then we would not know if it was the noise or the heat that was responsible for any difference.

It is also possible that uncontrolled variables could conceal the real effects of an independent variable. For example, for all we know, the students in our experiment might be helped by being in a cool (as opposed to a hot) room but put off by being in a noisy (compared to a quiet) room. If the noisy room was cool and the quiet room hot, then we might find that there was, in the end, no overall difference between the performance of the two groups of students. Clearly, in this case, the conclusion that the lack of difference between the two groups meant that there was no measurable effect of noise would be mistaken.

In our imaginary experiment on the effects of noise on exam performance it is important to note that, in order to see if presence of noise affects performance, we must test the performance of subjects on the same task under an *experimental* condition with noise and a *control* condition with no noise. Subjects performing under the control condition should be performing in *exactly the same circumstances* as those under the experimental condition with the exception that they are not subject to noise. In this way, given that it is a well designed study and effects of variation in the independent variable produce measurable change in the dependent variable, then the experimenter can conclude that it could only have been caused by one thing—the presence or absence of noise.

By "exactly the same circumstances" we mean that the experimental environments are the same and that the subjects performing under each of the conditions are equivalent. The first of these requirements is usually easier to establish than the second. Experimenters attempt to achieve equivalence of the subjects by two main methods—either by *matching* or by *random allocation*. Matching involves pairing each of the subjects in the control group with a subject in the experimental condition. Each pair of subjects is matched on all, or at least all of the known or suspected, factors that might affect their performance. Thus, it is common to match for such things as age and IQ, which could affect performance in a wide range of situations. There might be other characteristics of the subjects—unknown to the experimenter—that affect their behaviour. If, in our imaginary experiment, subjects with hearing difficulties were allocated to the noise condition then we might anticipate that the effects of noise on performance might be somewhat obscured. Random allocation of subjects to conditions prevents unmatched factors from having any systematic effect on the outcome of the experiment. The thinking behind random allocation is that if subjects are allocated entirely randomly to the different conditions of the experiment, then it will be unlikely (though not entirely impossible) that any characteristics of the subjects will confound the manipulation of the independent variable. (Any extraneous factor that does affect the dependent variable is called a confounding factor.) If subjects are allocated randomly to conditions then any subjects with hearing difficulties would be expected to be evenly distributed across the conditions of the experiment. Matching and random allocation are therefore two important procedures that are used to help rule out possible alternative explanations of the observed effects on a dependent measure.

Sometimes, instead of comparing two groups of subjects, one group of subjects serves both as control and experimental group. In what are called *repeated measures* or *within-subject* designs (see Chapter 3) observations are taken of the dependent variable under experimental and control conditions. In our imaginary experiment we would compare the performance of students who did an exam under both noise and no-noise conditions. Plainly, if you asked students to do the same exam twice one might expect that they would approach it rather differently the second time around! There are a number of problems—and recommended remedies—for designing within-subject designs so that one can make valid inferences about the influence of the independent variable (see Chapter 3).

In practice it is often very difficult to be sure that all variables that might affect the dependent variable have been controlled, but an attempt is made to control as many as possible. In summary, the ideal experiment is a tightly controlled study that is organised precisely so that the effects of changes in the independent variable on the dependent variable can be assessed and the range of possible explanations can be kept to a minimum.

The correlational study:
Passive observation

Experiments are just one of the methods for attempting to make inferences about causal relationships between variables. There is also a method that can be applied to data collected by passive observation rather than by active experimentation. It is possible for the researcher simply to observe passively the relationship between measures of two variables—without attempting to manipulate the variables of interest or attempting to control the influence of any other variables. The simple correlational study is concerned with measuring the strength of association between two variables. For example, it would be possible to measure the level of aggressiveness in a sample of children and record their television viewing habits. On doing so we might find that the level of aggressiveness shown by children is positively correlated with the number of violent television programmes that they watch. Consequently, in this imaginary example, we could conclude that children who watch more violent programmes tend to be more aggressive.

In its simplest form the correlational study does not allow one to say much about what caused what. If one observes a correlation between two variables A and B then A may cause B; B may cause A; or some other variable may cause them both. In relation to our example we can see that this leaves three general possibilities regarding the cause of the observed association between aggressiveness and viewing violent television programmes. It might be that watching violent programmes causes children to be violent —perhaps by a process of imitation or by being over-stimulated. Alternatively the direction of causality might be the other way around; for example, it is possible that naturally aggressive children tend to be more interested in watching violent programmes. A third possibility is that some other factor is responsible for both aggressiveness in children and their television-viewing habits. For example one could speculate that perhaps some of these children were reared in such a way as to render them both more aggressive *and* more interested in viewing violent television. A combination of any two or even all three of these possibilities might be responsible for the observed correlation. Moreover, there will often be more than one possible explanation for each of these three general categories of possibilities. Thus, if watching violent programmes causes children to be aggressive, it might be due to imitation or it might be as a result of increased anxiety caused by viewing the violence.

In correlational studies, the researcher does not manipulate an independent variable and observe the resulting effect on a dependent variable. The researcher simply passively observes the relationship between a pair or pairs of variables. Thus, correlational studies do not have control groups, nor can the researcher randomly assign subjects to conditions. Indeed, dependent and independent variables cannot be distinguished. For these reasons a statistical measure of correlation cannot be taken to indicate the nature of the causal relationship between the two variables. As we have seen in our simple example there are various possible causal relationships that might underlie the discovery of a correlation.

If you are a little disheartened by this difficulty with correlation you might be sympathetic with Pearl (1997) who has recently been critical of the inability of statistics to provide researchers with procedures that enable them to measure causality directly. Pearl argues that the development of the concept of correlation in statistics has rather held back the development of methods for analysing causality. Presentation of the argument requires a brief historical excursion. One of the people most responsible for the development of modern statistics was Karl Pearson who was a student of Galton—the person who first discovered correlation (Galton, 1888). Pearson was so impressed by the discovery of correlation that he thought it ought to replace the whole notion of cause and effect. In the third edition of his book, *The Grammar of Science*, Pearson wrote a new chapter entitled "Contingency and Correlation—the insufficiency of causation" (Pearson, 1911). Introducing this new topic Pearson wrote (1911, p.xii): "Beyond such discarded topics as 'matter' and 'force' lies still another fetish amidst the inscrutable arcana of modern science, namely, the category of cause and effect". Pearson specifically denied the need for a concept of causal relation beyond the correlation, a view he held throughout his life. According to Pearl (1997), his rejection of causality was so fierce and Pearson's influence so great that causation was exterminated from statistics before it had a chance to take root.

According to Pearl (1997) this attitude to causality prevails in statistical texts to the present day. For example, the *Encyclopedia of Statistical Science* (Kotz & Johnson, 1982) devotes 12 pages to correlation but only 2 pages to causation, and spends one of those pages demonstrating that "correlation does not imply causation". Similarly, most modern statisticians treat causality as a problem that statistical techniques are simply not designed to address. Dawid (1979, p.30) states: "causal inference is one of the most important, most subtle, and most neglected of all the problems of statistics". Speed (1990, p.58) advises: "considerations of causality should be treated as they have always been treated in statistics: preferably not at all, but if necessary, then with very great care". Cox and Wermuth (1996, p.219) admitted: "We have not in this book used the words *causal* or *causality* ... Our reason for caution is that it is rare that firm conclusions about causality can be drawn from one study, however carefully designed and executed, especially when the study is observational". Pearl (1997) claims that this caution and avoidance has had a debilitating effect on researchers looking to statistics for guidance.

Causal inferences are often made on the basis of observed correlations however and, moreover, can be made validly. How valid such inferences are depends on the satisfaction of three commonly accepted conditions. First there must be evidence of time precedence. For A to be a possible cause of B, A must occur before B in time. Second, there must be evidence of a relationship—the two variables must be, to some degree, associated or correlated. Third, the correlation must be non-spurious. This means that there must not be a third variable that causes both A and B. For example, in a sample of children one might find that height correlates with mathematical ability. However, before speculating on how being tall could improve mathematical ability, it might be as well to consider the fact that height correlates with age! Older children would be expected to do better than younger children on most tests of ability. However, providing we have measures of other relevant variables, we can use methods of *partial correlation* that "partial out" the effects of third variables on the correlation of interest. Thus, if we knew how old all the children were in our sample then we could partial out the effects of age in the sample to see if a correlation still exists between two variables such as height and mathematical ability when the association with age is taken into account.

When discovering a correlation between two variables it often seems quite temptingly obvious that one must be the cause of the other. Such a temptation should be resisted, however, until all other possible causal relationships have been eliminated. Consider how different our educational system might be for example if it had been concluded that superior height in children was directly responsible for superior mathematical ability. Sometimes the matter of locating causality will be difficult. Often it will be necessary for the researcher to attempt to discern a plausible causal link—for instance rioting cannot plausibly be the cause of hot weather but hot weather may be one cause of rioting.

One advantage of the correlational approach is that it enables the psychologist to escape from the laboratory and investigate data that were not collected in the laboratory but that represent behaviour that occurred naturally in the real world. A common criticism of laboratory experiments is that they can affect the very behaviour being measured—when people know they are being observed they may behave differently (see Chapter 2). Data representing real-world behaviour collected outside the laboratory can be investigated using correlational methods.

Sometimes the study of data from the real world outside the rigorously controlled laboratory can open up fascinating opportunities for psychological study. For example, when studying allegations of political bias in television news, Mullen et al. (1986) found that the main newscaster on one channel tended to smile more frequently when mentioning one particular candidate. The other main newscasters on other channels did not show this bias. Could the biased newscaster influence viewers' attitudes and even their voting behaviour? Mullen et al. conducted a telephone survey to investigate whether voting behaviour was associated with which nightly news programme was watched. They found that voters who regularly watched the newscaster with the biased facial expression were significantly more likely to vote for the candidate that the newscaster had smiled upon. As the title of their paper asked, can a smile elect a president? Mullen et al. carefully considered three possible explanations for their finding. Either viewing the newscaster's biased facial expressions caused the viewer's voting preferences, or perhaps the viewer's voting preferences caused them to view the newscaster who had the biased expression, or some other unknown third variable accounted for the results.

Another advantage of correlational methods is that one can explore data concerning issues that it would not be ethically possible to investigate experimentally (see Chapter 7). For example, psychologists who are interested in the effects of damage to particular areas of the human brain are not ethically able to selectively damage a sample of human brains. However, by keeping records of patients who have brain damage it is possible to study the association between damage to a particular area of the brain and particular behaviours. Similarly, while it might be possible to observe an association between long-term maternal deprivation during infancy and delinquency during adolescence, it would not be ethical to *allocate* a group of infants to a condition where they were deprived of their mothers. Of course an experimental design permits greater control over the influence of other variables but the advantages of active manipulation of variables carry with them a moral duty to act responsibly.

SUMMARY
The correlational
approach

Correlational studies allow analysis of behaviour that has been passively observed—rather than collected under experimentally rigorously controlled conditions.

- Determining the cause of a correlation between variables requires special care. If two variables A and B are correlated then there are three possible causal interpretations:

  (i) A may be the cause of B;

  (ii) B may be the cause of A;

  (iii) Some other variable may cause A and B.

- Correlational studies can be used to investigate behaviour occurring outside the laboratory which it might not be ethical or practically possible to observe under laboratory conditions.

Experimental and correlational approaches: A comparison

Whereas the experimenter is interested in the variation he creates by manipulating variables, the correlator is interested in the variation already existing between individuals and/or groups of individuals within or across cultures. The correlator's aim is to understand the variance produced by nature. For the experimental psychologist individual differences in the subjects of the study are often seen as a problem rather than a focus of interest. A large amount of variation obtained between subjects within a treatment condition is seen as an indication that the experimenter has not controlled the experiment tightly enough. In experimental studies individual variation is termed "error variance" and is one source of variation that the experimenter will deliberately try to eliminate by matching subjects or using homogeneous subject groups.

In psychological research the correlator's main interest is usually individual variation so, in order to produce the maximum possible variation between people, heterogeneous samples are often used. The correlational approach is at the heart of *psychometrics*—the measurement and theory of individual differences. In research using the correlational approach no attempt is made to change the extent to which an individual or group of individuals exhibits a certain behaviour or possesses a certain disposition or competence. Variation is produced by studying individuals who differ or who are expected to differ on the feature of interest. Thus, if we are interested in the association between anxiety and performance of some task we might observe people who are known to vary in levels of anxiety. The correlator would typically design a questionnaire to measure the levels of anxiety in people (see Chapter 5) and then look for a correlation with the behaviour of interest. By contrast, the experimenter's approach to this issue would be to attempt to manipulate anxiety in subjects and observe the effects on performance of the task.

It should be clear from this discussion that the experiment is the primary approach used within an *explanatory research strategy*. The correlational approach is typical of a *descriptive research strategy*. Data collection in the experimental approach tends to involve measures of performance (e.g. number of words recalled) under different task conditions (e.g. with and without interference from noise). The correlational approach tends to involve data collected from surveys, interviews, or questionnaires. Under these two different approaches the analysis of these data is also rather different. Data analysis in the experimental format typically involves looking for differences in performance under different conditions, while the correlational approach uses statistics that evaluate correlation and association.

The theoretical perspectives associated with these two perspectives are also rather different. The experimental approach tends to be concerned with the search for general laws of behaviour that apply to all people, whereas the correlational approach is characterised by an attempt to measure and theorise about the nature of the differences between individuals or groups of people. Thus, the experimental psychologist manipulating levels of anxiety—perhaps by telling an experimental sample of student subjects that they face a surprise statistics exam in half an hour—might discover that they are less able to solve anagrams than a control group who are not told about an impending exam. This would support a conclusion that anxiety impedes the solving of anagrams. The correlator on the other hand might measure levels of anxiety in a sample of subjects and then attempt to measure the association between levels of anxiety in individuals and their ability to solve anagrams. If he or she were to discover such an association then the correlator would have evidence consistent with the view that *anxious people* are less able to solve anagrams. Note that the experimenter's conclusion is very general—it says nothing about how different people might respond. The correlator's conclusion, on the other hand, is focused on individual differences and does not propose any account of how anxiety might affect people in general.

These two approaches to research are often pursued by different groups of psychologists; so much so that Cronbach (1957, 1975) has termed them "the two disciplines of scientific psychology". Experimental psychologists rarely concern themselves with individual differences whereas researchers exploring individual differences have tended to overlook the influence of external situational variables on behaviour (Mischel, 1968). Plainly, an approach to psychological research that acknowledges the influence of both individual differences and of external factors is preferable to an approach that ignores the existence of one or another of these sorts of factors.

SUMMARY
Experimental
versus
correlational
approaches

- The experimental approach is typically interested in psychological factors that affect all people—the commonalities of people rather than the differences among them.
- Correlational approaches are commonly used to explore individual differences. The correlational approach is central to investigations of personality.
- Data analysis in the experimental format typically involves looking for differences in performance under different conditions while the correlational approach uses statistics that evaluate correlation and association.
- The two different approaches have been identified with different theoretical accounts. Experimental psychologists tend to emphasise the influence of variables on people whereas correlational psychologists emphasise variations between people. The two approaches would be more usefully seen as complementary.

The analysis of experimental and correlational studies

Finally, this chapter ends with a consideration of the methods of analysis associated with experiments and correlations. Very often students using questionnaires will concentrate on correlational analyses when analysing the results of their studies whereas those conducting experiments will use measures of difference between conditions. However, it should be noted that measures of correlation can be usefully reported for experimental studies and measures of difference can be useful for analysing questionnaires.

In a within-subject or repeated measures experiment it is possible to report a measure of the correlation in performance for the subjects in the control and experimental conditions. It may well be that the effects of the independent variable, although measurably significant, are not consistent across all the subjects. Imagine an experiment, designed to examine the effects of noise on performance of a mental task, where the subjects attempt to solve a series of arithmetic problems in an experimental condition with loud noise and a control condition of relative quiet. Although the noise might be shown to be generally detrimental by a measure of the difference between the two conditions, it might affect some people more than others; it is possible that some of the subjects are not affected by the noise—or even benefit from it. A measure of the correlation between performance under the two conditions would tell us the extent to which the subjects were similarly affected by the noise.

When using a questionnaire it is perfectly reasonable to report a measure of the difference in response between different groups of subjects—males and females, or people from two different cultures for example. However, we would warn against one application of difference tests that is, sadly, rather popular among students conducting laboratory experiments. It is *not* recommended that you treat a measure of individual difference—say extroversion—as if it were an independent variable by testing a group of subjects and then classifying them as high or low in extroversion and then comparing the performance of the two groups of different subjects on some task.

Although this strategy appears on the face of it to be quite reasonable, it represents a confusion between the experimental and correlational approaches. As people have not been assigned at random to the two "conditions" they will differ in respect not just of extroversion but of any other variables that are correlated with extroversion. Another reason why this approach is inappropriate is because a lot of information will have been needlessly ignored. If, instead of splitting the subjects into two groups, a correlation between extroversion and task performance was calculated then all the measured variation in extroversion is evaluated—not just the differences represented by the simple dichotomy between "high" and "low".

For example, consider the following experiment and set of data. One group of subjects was administered a questionnaire which tested for their self-esteem. The scores on the questionnaire were all recorded. As the experimenter was interested in the relation between self-esteem and motivation to succeed, each of the subjects was then individually asked to complete a newspaper crossword "as well as they could". Unbeknown to the subjects although the crossword consisted of mainly very easy clues it also had several unsolvable clues. As a measure of motivation the experimenter simply recorded the amount of time that the subjects spent on the crossword before they gave up. The scores for self-esteem (where 30 was the maximum possible score) and the time in minutes spent on the crossword are given in Table 4.1.

Now it would be possible to allocate the subjects into two groups on the basis of their self-esteem scores and compare those subjects with low self-esteem with those with high self-esteem. We could split them into two equal groups by separating the subjects with the highest scores from those with the lowest—subjects 1 to 6 have lower scores than subjects 7 to 12.

If we did this then we would have two sets of scores, so we could then compare the crossword times for the two groups with statistical tests. We would then be examining if the subjects categorised as being of high self-esteem had different crossword times to those categorised as being of low self-esteem. But notice that by doing this we are considering that our subjects can only have two levels of self-esteem—high or low. In fact, as you can see from the scores in the table, there is a wide range of self-esteem scores. If, instead of measuring the differences between two artificially created groups, we measured the correlation between self-esteem and crossword time the full range of self-esteem would be taken into account. Moreover, by reporting a correlation in this manner we do not risk creating the impression that we had somehow, using the experimental method, allocated subjects randomly to high and low self-esteem conditions.

TABLE 4.1
The crossword study

Subject No.	1	2	3	4	5	6	7	8	9	10	11	12
Self-esteem	5	8	8	10	11	13	14	14	15	20	22	26
Crossword time (in minutes)	3	3	6	5	7	5	8	6	7	7	6	8

As a function of thinking about the methods associated with the experimental approach to psychology, valuable opportunities for applying correlational methods can be missed. It follows that researchers should think through carefully what different methods of investigation and analysis can offer in terms of insights into the causes of behaviour. The consequences of not recognising the value—and the limitations—of the correlational approach can be (and indeed have been) far reaching.

Exercises

1. Design a study that will enable you to test the hypothesis that there are individual differences in levels of stress (measured by a questionnaire) that are correlated with individual differences in the performance of a skilled task under time pressure.

2. Imagine that you have data indicating the reading vocabularies of 30 pairs of 12-year-old identical twins who had been separated at birth. They were reared either in a home with foster parents with high socio-economic status, or in a home with foster parents with low socio-economic status. Consider what sort of inferences might be made by measuring the correlation between the pairs of twins. What inferences could be made by comparing the differences between the twins in the two different environments?

References

Cox, D., & Wermuth, N. (1996). *Multivariate dependencies—models analyses and interpretation*. London: Chapman & Hall.

Cronbach, L.J. (1957). The two disciplines of scientific psychology. *American Psychologist, 12*, 671–684.

Cronbach, L.J. (1975). Beyond the two disciplines of scientific psychology. *American Psychologist, 30*, 116–127.

Dawid, P. (1979). Conditional independence in statistical theory. *Journal of the Royal Statistical Society, Series B, 41*, 1–31.

Galton, F. (1888). Co-relations and their measurement, chiefly from anthropological data. *Proceedings of the Royal Society of London, 45*, 135–145.

Kotz, S. and Johnson, N.L.(Eds.) (1982). *Encyclopedia of statistical sciences*. New York: John Wiley & Sons.

Mischel, W. (1968). *Personality and assessment*. New York: John Wiley & Sons.

Mullen, B., Futrell, D., Stairs, D., Tice, D.M., Baumeister, R.F., Dawson, K.E., Riordan, C.A., Radloff, C.E., Goethals, G.R., Kennedy, J.G., & Rosenfield, P. (1986). Newscasters' facial expressions and voting behaviour of viewers: Can a smile elect a president? *Journal of Personality and Social Psychology, 51*, 291–295.

Pearl, J. (1997). *The new challenge: From a century of statistics to the age of causation*. Technical report R-249. Computer Science Department. University of California at Los Angeles.

Pearson, K. (1911). *Grammar of science* (3rd edn.). London: A. & C. Black.

Speed, T. (1990). Complexity, calibration and causality in influence diagrams. In R. Oliver & J. Smith (Eds.), *Influence diagrams, belief nets and decision analysis*. New York: John Wiley & Sons.

Questionnaire design 5

Ingrid Schoon

Aims

The aim of this chapter is to introduce the reader to the major stages in questionnaire design and to demonstrate how to choose and develop a questionnaire for a research project. Areas covered include: functions of the questionnaire, questionnaire planning, modes of data collection, response format, question wording, layout of a questionnaire, and the criteria used to evaluate the quality of a questionnaire (reliability and validity).

Introduction: The function of a questionnaire

The questionnaire is a widely used and well respected instrument in psychological research. The questionnaire is basically a tool for data collection. The major advantages of the questionnaire in comparison to other research tools, for example the experiment or the unstructured interview, are its obvious simplicity, its versatility, and its low cost as a method of data collection. No fancy or complicated apparatus is needed to administer a questionnaire—paper and pencil will do. However, questionnaires can also be administered via computer-assisted techniques. Or, in cases where one wants to reach a great number of people, or individuals who live in widely dispersed areas, one might consider using a postal questionnaire. The mode of data collection (see later section) should depend on its appropriateness to the research question and the means and resources at your disposal.

Questionnaires are used in large-scale surveys, such as the British Social Attitudes Survey (Jowell et al., 1993), as well as in smaller-scale projects, including psychology laboratory classes. Questionnaires are used to gather facts about individuals, such as their age, gender, level of education, status of employment, their eating habits, etc., or if one wants to assess a phenomenon that is not directly observable, or cannot be experimentally manipulated, for example loss of self-esteem in response to unemployment. The data collected from a well designed questionnaire is commonly considered to be of good enough quality for generating or testing hypotheses (Cronbach, 1990; Oppenheim, 1992). Questionnaire construction furthermore is employed in the development of psychometric tests that are used for assessing personality characteristics, attitudes, abilities, or aptitudes.

Generating hypotheses

If a new topic is explored it is best to use a number of open-ended questions (see the later section on "Response format") to find out how people talk about it and what aspects are important to them. A questionnaire study can give information about the range of likely responses and a description of how common certain responses are.

Test development

Based on the information collected in an exploratory study one could then consider developing a more specific test, or scale, which is made up of many questions (also called items) all assessing the same phenomenon. The formulation and selection of appropriate items is a time-consuming and laborious process, based on an intensive literature review, and possibly interviews. Items have to be composed and piloted, improved, revised, refined, and then piloted again. The final version of a test is then administered to a great number of individuals, and the items are tested as to whether they do indeed measure what they intend to measure, and whether the questionnaire measures a psychological phenomenon reliably and accurately (see criteria for judging the quality of a questionnaire).

Hypothesis testing

Once a valid and reliable test has been developed it can be applied in a variety of areas. Tests are used for assessing personality characteristics, abilities, aptitudes, attitudes, and interests. They are used for classification and diagnosis, for example in career guidance or in a clinical setting, for the evaluation of existing programmes (for example the effect of relaxation training on exam performance), or generally for scientific enquiry and model testing.

Thus the simple questionnaire can be applied at different levels of investigation and different levels of complexity. One has to be aware that each of these objectives should be dealt with separately, and that each step has to build on a prior one.

- The questionnaire is a tool for data collection.
- The questionnaire is used for:
  generating hypotheses;
  test development;
  testing hypotheses.

SUMMARY
The function of a questionnaire.

Questionnaire planning

Any questionnaire is developed for a particular purpose in a given context, and will be administered to a particular set of people at a specific time. Before even the most initial thoughts about the nature and structure of the questionnaire are put to paper, one should ensure that one has a clear understanding of the particular research question. A lack of clarity at this basic level will result in uncertainty about what concepts need to be measured or what information should be collected. It is often impossible, or extremely expensive, to go back to respondents and clarify unasked questions.

Questionnaire specification

The function of a questionnaire is to measure something. What a questionnaire measures should be contained in the questionnaire specification. The detailed specification of measurement aims must be precisely and logically related to the aims of the overall research plan. In many cases we start off with only a rather general idea of what it is we want to measure. Consider for example the case of scholastic achievement where topics like "spelling" and "arithmetic" seem reasonably concrete and definable. Does spelling ability refer to the skill of arranging letters in the right order or filling in missing letters—and are these exactly the same skills? Does spelling mean being able to recognise misprints? Does it include the ability to learn how to spell? It is unlikely that one single test can measure precisely all these things and so one can imagine the difficulties in attempting to measure things that are less precisely understood.

To lay down the detailed specifications for a questionnaire is not an easy task. It requires a lot of reading, planning, a proper research design, and the conceptualisation of the research problem. If, for example, one wishes to assess the relationship between extraversion and risk-taking behaviour among teenagers, how will this issue be operationalised in practice and what measures are required? Sometimes items from existing instruments can be used, but one has to check whether these instruments have been developed for adults only and whether they are really suitable for a teenage population. Furthermore, crucial aspects, like willingness to take social, financial, and/or physical risks, should be covered appropriately, otherwise one would need different questions.

The development of a questionnaire takes time and skill. Experience all too often shows that almost any researcher believes they can design a questionnaire, with the result that the analysis stage is reached before the discovery of irresolvable problems. It is not enough to write plain English and to have good common sense to produce a good questionnaire. A well constructed questionnaire is more than a haphazard collection of questions, but is carefully designed and structured, taking into consideration (a) the research question, (b) the characteristics of the respondent, (c) ways of asking appropriate questions, and (d) the available resources (time and money).

Question content

We can differentiate factual (objective) and non-factual (subjective) types of questions. *Factual questions* are supposed to have a "true" answer that is verifiable. For example, you can ask the respondent to give a correct response to:

- Questions about facts that are necessary to classify the response according to a number of criteria, so-called *classification* questions (age, sex, marital status, income, education, occupation, and so on).
- *Behavioural* questions (for example: "Do you ever go to watch a movie in the cinema ... yes or no?"; or "Do you read a newspaper every day ... yes or no?").
- *Knowledge* questions ("The earth is round ... true or false?"; or "The capital of France is Bordeaux ... right or wrong?").

Non-factual or subjective questions, on the other hand, are more difficult to verify as they deal with aspects of the state of mind of the respondent, such as questions regarding beliefs, attitudes, opinions.

For example:

- Married men are happier than unmarried men. (Please tick one answer) True [ ] Untrue [ ]
- Men and women should do the same jobs around the house. (Please tick one answer) Always [ ] Sometimes [ ] Never [ ]
- Most people are honest and well intentioned. (Please tick one answer) Do you agree [ ] or disagree [ ]

Subjective questions are generally more complex and multifaceted than factual questions. However, they also assume a "true", relatively stable attitude, or personality characteristic, just as factual questions do. But in approximating this "true value" one has to use more than one question, just as a medical doctor would use more than one question to find out exactly what a patient is suffering from.

Sufficient awareness of these different question "types" should steer researchers' thinking toward a systematic development of a set of questions for use in a questionnaire. If researchers are unclear as to the type of questions they are asking, they run the considerable risk of transforming their lack of clarity into the collection of the wrong type of data. Besides the type of questions to be used the researcher must also be clear about the characteristics of the respondent.

The respondent

Will the questionnaire be addressed to an adult sample or to children? Will it be a large sample or a small one? Will the respondents be housewives, company directors, relatives of cancer patients, primary school children, students, or a random sample of the entire population? Will the same respondents be approached more than once (then one has to ask for their name and address)? Does one intend to keep the respondents anonymity (then one cannot ask for their name and address)? Is our research topic subject to seasonal fluctuations (e.g. tourism)?

In order for your questionnaire to be successful you have to find ways of gaining the respondents' cooperation and of motivating them to respond to your questions. The respondent must be able to understand the question, s/he must be willing to answer the question, and s/he must have the knowledge to answer the question (De Lamater, 1982; Groves, 1989, Tourangeau, 1984). One also has to consider that some questions, particularly questions about private and sensitive issues, cannot be asked without clarifying ethical aspects first (see Chapter 7).

Understanding the question

Comprehension of a question is primarily a function of question wording. The question should indicate clearly which level of detail is required, it should be clear, simple, and relevant to all respondents. It is a tricky business to find the right words to convey specific meanings that are equivalent to each respondent, and to elicit truthful and accurate responses. However much we try to standardise our questioning procedures in order to create "stimulus equivalence", there will always remain differences in the way in which questions are understood by each respondent. For example, in the seemingly straightforward question "How many times did you disagree with your partner about how to spend your spare time during the past week?", the respondent must decide what exactly constitutes disagreement (does it mean differences in opinion, or physical quarrel?) and about spending spare time (does it include taking a bath?). Keeping these difficulties in mind, a number of researchers have developed guidelines of how to formulate questions in order to overcome these problems (see question wording). However, we not only have to take care that our questions can be understood, we also have to make sure that the respondent has the relevant information or knowledge to answer the question accurately.

Knowledgeable respondents

Only respondents who have the necessary knowledge to answer the questions should be included in a questionnaire study, and the ones who do not are to be excluded. For example, respondents answering a questionnaire about their current satisfaction in a relationship or marriage, should be in a relationship or marriage. We furthermore have to make sure the respondent accurately recalls information, for example, dates and frequencies of their eating habits. Research has shown that recent events are remembered with greater accuracy than earlier events (Groves, 1989). Thus questions should give a relevant time frame ("How many digestive biscuits did you consume yesterday?"—instead of "How many digestive biscuits did you consume within the past month?") and not overestimate the memory span of the respondent. One could also provide "cues" to aid the reconstruction of events, and ask the respondent explicitly to think about all occasions on which they ate their biscuits.

Willingness to respond

Even after having understood the question, and being able to answer the question, the respondent might not be willing to answer adequately. For example, the willingness of the respondent to cooperate can be diminished by the degree to which questions affect private or self-incriminating information (for example, drunken driving, drug taking, bankruptcy). Furthermore the respondent might evaluate the level of accuracy required by a question and/or its social acceptability. Respondents might be reluctant to reveal that they possess socially undesirable traits (for example, having no sense of humour, or being a racist), and they might decide either to omit or to under-report them. On the other hand, respondents may be more affected by the desire to help the researcher (conformity) and over-report, or give an affirmative "yes" to each question (acquiescence). Or they might simply be too tired to respond. In no case should a respondent be forced to respond to a questionnaire, and his or her right to withdraw from the study at any time has to be respected.

Besides question type and respondent characteristics one should consider the way in which the analysis of the collected data will be approached. There is little point in designing a questionnaire that becomes clumsy to administer and/or cannot produce the appropriate data for analysis. The time spent on planning at the early stages of a project is time well invested. Nonetheless, it is very often the case that the importance of the planning stage is underestimated. No researcher should ever assume that the design they produce cannot be improved upon. Individual questions, the questionnaire as

---

- What are you going to ask?
- Will you require factual information and/or subjective data on individual states of mind?
- Do your questions tap into sensitive areas?
- Can the respondent understand the question?
- What does your respondent know?
- Is the respondent willing to answer the question?
- Is the response likely to be accurate?

SUMMARY
Planning your questionnaire.

a whole, or the initial approach may not work in the way envisaged. Once the main stage of administering a structured questionnaire is in progress, there is little that can be done to correct mistakes.

Once one has decided on these points, the next step in constructing a questionnaire is to think about the most appropriate method of data collection.

Modes of data collection

There are different methods of collecting questionnaire data, and each has its specific advantages and disadvantages (see Bourque & Fiedler, 1995; Converse & Presser, 1986; Oppenheim 1992; Sudman & Bradburn, 1982). In the broadest sense the term questionnaire covers the range of:

a. self-administered or group-administered questionnaires;
b. postal questionnaires;
c. structured interview schedules, including face-to-face and telephone interviews.

Self-administered questionnaires

Self-administered questionnaires are one of the most frequently used methods for collecting data. A self-administered questionnaire is usually presented to the respondent by an interviewer or by someone in an official position, such as the researcher, a teacher, a hospital receptionist, or a psychological assistant. The purpose of the inquiry is explained, and then the respondent is left alone to complete the questionnaire on his or her own, and the questionnaire will be picked up later. This method of data collection ensures a high response rate, accurate sampling, and minimum of interviewer bias, while permitting interviewer assessment (additional information from observing the reaction of the respondent). In case of difficulties with the instrument necessary explanations can be provided, giving the benefit of direct personal contact. This type of questionnaire can also be administered via computer-assisted techniques.

Group-administered questionnaires

These, in contrast, are not distributed on an individual basis but are given to groups of respondents assembled together, such as school children or invited audiences. They are used in a wide variety of contexts, ranging from classroom tests in schools to personality assessment in a psychiatric clinic. The advantages of this type of questionnaire are similar to the self-administered version, and allow for a degree of personal contact and thus the opportunity to correct misunderstandings and to check for completeness. On the other hand, they are not usable with general populations and are restricted to individuals assembling at a certain venue, such as a school or hospital. There might be additional problems with members of the group influencing each other and individual timing of responses. Variations of this procedure can involve computer-assisted presentation, or the use of slides or a film, or having questions read aloud while respondents write their answers in a booklet. The last procedure ensures that respondents answer the questions in the same order and that all respondents have the same amount of time to do so.

Thus self- and group-administered questionnaires are generally completed in the presence of an official agent, supervisor, or researcher. However, sometimes questionnaires are completed by the respondent without a supervisor or other monitoring agent being present. The most common example of unsupervised administration is the mail or postal questionnaire.

Mail or postal questionnaires

Like the self-administered questionnaire the postal questionnaire is widely used. It involves low costs in data collection and data analysis, and can be used to reach individuals that live in widely dispersed areas. When a questionnaire is administered in a completely unsupervised manner, it is essential that the questionnaire is completely self-sufficient and self-explanatory. No research staff is available to answer questions or to ensure that the respondent understands the questions, nor that the correct person completes the questionnaire.

The structured interview schedule

The interview, unlike most other techniques, requires interpersonal skills. For example, putting the respondent at ease, establishing a good rapport, keeping up the motivation of the respondent, noting down the responses without upsetting the conversational flow, and giving support without introducing bias. Furthermore the interview situation is partly determined by the characteristics and expectations of the interviewer: age, gender, dress, etc. These characteristics can create biases and distortions of which we must be aware (for more details see Oppenheim, 1992; Rosenthal, 1976)

Interviews often have a higher response rate than the postal questionnaire. They offer the researcher the opportunity to correct misunderstandings and to carry out observations and ratings while ensuring that each question is answered in the right sequence. Interviewers can often succeed with respondents who have reading or language difficulties. On the other hand, interviews are expensive and time-consuming to conduct and to process, there are always the risks of interviewer bias, and interviews are usually too expensive to reach a widely dispersed sample.

Each of the three major questionnaire types has advantages and disadvantages (see Table 5.1). The final choice of an instrument will depend on its appropriateness to the purpose (research idea) and the means at your disposal (time, money, training).

For example, a group-administered questionnaire is the appropriate choice, if the researcher aims for a high response rate, low costs in data collection and data analysis, if s/he considers moderate

	Standardised interview	Postal, self-admin questionnaire	Group-admin questionnaire
Response rate	high	low	high
Cost of data collection	high	low	low
Cost of data processing	high	low	low
Personal contact	high	low	possible
Correction of misunderstanding	yes	no	possible
Control over q. sequence	yes	no	possible
Check for incompleteness	yes	no	possible
Possible bias	high	some	some
Suited for illiterate people	yes	no	possible
Ability to reach widely dispersed respondents	difficult	yes	possible difficult

TABLE 5.1
Advantages and disadvantages of the major types of questionnaire.

personal contact as sufficient in order to correct possible misunderstandings and to have control over question sequence and completeness. This type of questionnaire is also a possible choice if one wants to assess individuals who cannot read or write (for example young children), but cannot be used if the respondents live far away from each other and are not likely to assemble in the same venue.

Response format

There are different ways of formulating questions. At the simplest level, questions can be divided into either open or closed format. When respondents give answers in their own words, the question is open. When response alternatives are provided to the respondent, the question is closed.

Open questions

These questions are useful to tap into the views of the respondent and the ways they see the world. For example: "Imagine you have just won £1 million in the National Lottery. What would you do?", or "What does it mean to study something scientifically?". Questions are not followed by any kind of prefixed choice. The answers have to be recorded in full, and can be used as verbatim quotations or testimony. Open questions are informative about how respondents talk about an issue and what are salient aspects to them. Thus open questions are often used at an exploratory stage of research, when one wants to find out more about what respondents know about a topic or how they talk about it. However, respondents have to be highly motivated and/or verbally skilled to communicate their experiences and thoughts, and some respondents are reluctant to reveal detailed information, particularly on sensitive issues. Thus, open questions might be difficult to answer for some individuals. Open questions are furthermore difficult to code and analyse, and as such are considered as costly, time-consuming, and less reliable than closed questions.

Closed questions

When response alternatives are provided to the respondent, the question is closed. Closed questions are easy to process and analyse, requiring little time and low costs. On the other hand, closed questions require the researcher to have a reasonable idea of the likely and/or adequate response to the items in advance. Sometimes the offered alternatives are too crude or ill-chosen, and do not correspond to the respondent's true feelings or attitudes. They might even irritate the respondent, or bias the responses. Consider, for example, the following question:

Which of the following do you think is the most important problem facing this country today? Please tick only the most important problem:

[ ] Ordination of women priests
[ ] Pollution
[ ] Quality of public schools
[ ] Quality of health service
[ ] Energy shortage

Does any of the offered response alternatives correspond to your understanding of the most important problems facing this country today? Possibly not, but you might feel inclined to tick one of the boxes to comply with the question, and thus a biased response is created. As one can see from this example, good closed questions are difficult to develop. The available alternatives can create forced choices and rule out more adequate responses. Careful planning and pilot work can prevent such a situation. Sometimes it is also useful to ask the same question both in open and closed form.

The alternatives given to the respondent in a closed question may take several forms. The most commonly used types of response format are alternate choice items, multiple choice items, and rating scale items.

Alternate choice items

This question type gives the respondent two choices from which to select a response:

● The earth moves around the sun.
    True [ ] or false [ ]? (Please tick one answer)
● I really enjoy going to parties.
    Yes [ ] or no [ ]? (Please tick one answer)
● I prefer to work slowly but steadily.
    True [ ] or false [ ]? (Please tick one answer)

This type of question is fast and easy to use. It is most commonly used as a factual question, but can also be found in personality or attitude questionnaires. In the latter case the respondents often feel restricted by the narrow range of the response format, which forces them to choose an alternative that is not completely true or completely false, or where there are no right or wrong answers. However, sometimes the researcher wants the respondent to take sides and to indicate the alternative that is closest to their own perspective.

Multiple choice item

This is a question where the respondent is given more than two choices from which to select a response. This type of question consists of a statement or question and the different response options, of which one is correct or true.

> What is the capital of The Netherlands? (please circle one answer)
> a. Amsterdam
> b. The Hague
> c. Rotterdam
> d. Maastricht

This question type is most widely used for assessing facts and knowledge. Multiple choice questions are easy to administer and score, but sometimes it can be difficult to formulate equivalent or suitable response alternatives, particularly in knowledge questions, because each response alternative should be equally plausible.

Rating scale item

Rating scales ask the respondent to create an order by rating importance, endorsement, frequency, or intensity of their response on a scale. For example:

> Below are statements on some topics. To what extent do you agree or disagree with these statements? Please circle one number for each statement:

		Strongly agree	Agree	Disagree	Strongly disagree
1.	Marriage is for life	1	2	3	4
2.	Marriage gives you economic security	1	2	3	4
3.	A marriage without children is not fully complete	1	2	3	4

The endorsement items ranging from strongly agree to strongly disagree could be exchanged for other intensity items, such as definitely true, true, don't know, false, definitely false; or measures of frequency like never, rarely, sometimes, frequently, always. In principle the scale can range from 1 to 11. Most often, however, one will find a scale ranging from 1 to 5 (strongly agree, agree, uncertain, disagree, strongly disagree).

In designing a rating scale one has to consider the content of the choices (are they meaningful to the respondent), the number of choices (are they sufficient), whether to include a middle point and a "do not know" response. Sometimes it is useful to force the respondent to decide whether they are for or against something, and then the neutral middle option would not be included.

In principle all closed questions should be developed from open ones, except those where certain alternatives are the only possible ones, for example parties in an election, or daily national newspapers on sale. Open questions can be tested in various forms and then one can attempt to close them—this gives good insight and appreciation of the loss of information involved. Pilot work sometimes offers the possibility of closing quite subtle questions, thus avoiding expense and the possible distortion of coding.

Closed questions are the best option if one knows exactly what one is going to ask, if appropriate response options have been developed, if respondents are likely not to respond to a demanding questionnaire, and if data has to be collected and analysed quickly and at low cost. However, one has to be aware that the response options might limit or bias the response, and that sometimes it is useful to use both open and closed questions to assess a phenomenon accurately (see Table 5.2).

Question wording

The function of a question in a questionnaire is to elicit a particular communication. We hope that our respondents have certain information, ideas, or attitudes on the subject of our enquiry, and we want them to reveal this information with a minimum of distortion. Thus, the focus of a question must be right, the wording must be suitable and comprehensible, and the sequence and response categories (if any) must help the respondent without unintentionally biasing the answers.

Each question also has a covert function: to motivate the respondent to continue to cooperate. A question that strikes the respondent as rude, abstruse, or inconsiderate may affect not only their reply to that particular question but also their attitude to the next

TABLE 5.2
Purpose and
strengths and
weaknesses of
open versus
closed questions.

	Open question	Closed question

Purpose	– Exploration of new issues
	– Response categories are
	  unknown
		– Asking specific questions
		– Availability of prefixed
		  response choices

Response options	– Respondent uses own
	  words
	– Allow for free expression
	– Ability to obtain quotes and
	  testimony
		– Loss of spontaneity
		– Limitation of choice
		– Possibility of bias in answer
		  categories

Respondent	– Demands more effort (time,
	  knowledge, willingness to
	  write)
		– Less demanding
		– No bias towards the more
		  talkative respondent

Analysis	– Time-consuming	– Requires little time
Coding	– Costly and slow – May be unreliable	– Quick and easy – Sometimes too crude

Report	– Individual or grouped
	  responses
		– Statistical data (descriptive
		  statistics)

few questions and to the questionnaire as a whole. Basically, a question should be simple, intelligible and clear. If respondents do not understand the question, if the question is confusing, or asks something it was not intended to, then the question is essentially redundant. There is no cookbook with recipes of how to formulate questions that can be clearly understood, and that invite cooperation. Nevertheless, some authors have provided us with useful advice for good question wording (Converse & Presser, 1986; Fink, 1995; Fowler, 1995; Kline, 1986; Oppenheim, 1992; Payne, 1980; Sudman & Bradburn, 1982). Here is a short summary of the most common wording problems:

Simplicity

Simple language should be used wherever possible. Avoid jargon and technical terms, or if such terms are used, give clear explanations. On the other hand avoid being patronising or condescending!

Length of questions

Some authors suggest that questions should not contain more than 20 words: the shorter the better. However, it can be the case that by providing sufficient explanation the question is lengthened. Some researchers (Sudman & Bradburn, 1982) argue that extra length can sometimes pay off in that it allows the respondent to think and, thus, aids recall.

Avoidance of ambiguity

Make sure in the phrasing of the questions that you know what responses to the items mean. Consider, for example, the following question: "Have you suffered from headache or sickness lately?". What would a yes or no response to this question mean—does a yes indicate the person suffered from headache only but not from sickness, or did the respondent suffer from both? Thus you should avoid such ambiguous questions, or double negative questions, like: "Would you rather not use a biological washing powder?". Again, one should ask oneself what does a yes or no response to this question mean.

Furthermore, please keep in mind that some words are notorious for their ambiguity: For example, the simple question: "Do you have a car?" Does "you" mean yourself, your household, or family? Does "have" mean to own, to rent, or to have access to? You can improve these questions by specifying exactly what you mean: "Do you personally own a car?" Always give definitions of terms like often (at least once a week), occasionally (once or twice a month), hardly ever (once a year) to guarantee that a question is understood properly.

Leading questions

Questions that are worded in a particular way can create expectations and artificial opinions, and thus suggest to respondents that certain responses are appropriate and that others may be disapproved of. For example: "Would you agree that single mothers are treated unfairly in this country?", or "Do you agree that the National Lottery stimulates gambling among financially less well-off individuals?". These questions suggests to some people that you would like them to agree with you. Let respondents make up their minds for themselves.

Questionnaire layout

The appearance of a questionnaire is vital. There are many alternative ways of laying out a questionnaire, each of which can be equally appropriate. Basically a questionnaire should look inviting and be easy to fill in, with plenty of space for questions and answers. In designing a questionnaire one should pay attention to the kind of background information required, the appropriate instructions, how to lay out each question, and the sequencing of the questions (Bourque & Fiedler, 1995; Dillman, 1978; Oppenheim, 1992; Robson, 1993; Sudman & Bradburn, 1982).

Background information

Include headings and give a short description of the purpose of the questionnaire. This can help to make the questionnaire interesting to the respondent and stimulate his or her cooperation. You could also leave sufficient space for the respondent to fill in their personal data: their name, age, sex, income, level of education, or any other background information you require. It is often useful to obtain the date on which the questionnaire was completed—particularly so if it is to be administered again.

Instructions

Instructions must be clear and unambiguous. They should tell the respondent how to choose a response and how to indicate their response on the questionnaire. One can also indicate that all responses will be treated confidentially to increase the cooperation of the respondent. Serious loss of data can result from ambiguous or inadequate answering instructions. On self-administered questionnaires instructions should specify clearly the answering procedures: tick, circle, underline.

Layout of questions

It is important that questions are arranged on the page in a way that makes your questionnaire look inviting and easy to complete:

- Each question should be numbered.
- Do not cram too many questions on one page. Squeezing lots of items into a small space will make your form look dense, complex and uninviting, or might even confuse your respondents.
- If using more than one question type, group similar items together. Each type will need different instructions or response options.
- Questions should be justified to the left, and the response categories to the right, to create a clear visual relationship between each question and its response options.

- Be consistent with your response style (either tick, circle, or underline).
- Ensure that the typeface is clear and large enough to be easily read. One can use bold lettering or a different font for instructions or headings.
- When designing the layout of the questions think about how you are going to code the data for later data entry and analysis.

Sequencing

Start with easy questions and move on to the more difficult ones. Opening questions should be interesting, non-threatening (easy to answer), and motivate the respondent to cooperate and to complete the questionnaire. Generally it is advisable to start with relatively general, neutral questions that are not too difficult to answer. This should enable the respondent to "get into" the questionnaire. The first question should be congruent with the expectations of the respondent—if the respondent is asked to participate in a study on gender roles, s/he could be discouraged if the interview begins with questions about their recent salary.

Placement of sensitive and routine questions

It is best to avoid routine questions (for example questions on income, or religion), and sensitive questions (for example questions on drug abuse, domestic violence) in the beginning. Build up interest, trust, rapport before asking these questions! Some researchers argue that sensitive questions are best placed in the middle of the questionnaire—after a rapport has been developed and time is left to put questions into context. Do not end with sensitive questions—this will leave a bad impression and possible tension with the respondent. Generally, if sensitive questions have to be asked, ethical issues should be clarified before the administration of the questionnaire (see Chapter 7).

Balance of question types

Do not use too many open-ended questions (remember: they require a lot of writing, are time-consuming and costly to analyse). Open-ended questions can be placed at the end or middle or beginning of the questionnaire, depending on the context and sequencing of the other questions. Group all pre-coded questions according to their topics.

Order, flow, transition

After one has decided on opening and placement of routine and sensitive questions, the remaining topics have to be put into a reasonable order. Generally it is a good idea to collect questions concerning one topic all at once and not jump from one topic to the next and back again. Each new topic should be introduced with some transitional questions.

- A questionnaire should look inviting and easy to complete.
- Give a short description of the purpose of the questionnaire.
- Give clear and unambiguous instructions.
- Consider what background data is needed.
- Decide where to place routine and sensitive questions.
- Start with easy questions and move to more difficult ones.
- Group questions according to topic.
- If more than one question type is used, group similar items together.
- Use a minimum of open questions.
- Do not cram too many questions on one page.
- Consider carefully the layout, printing, choice of paper, and spacing of questions.

SUMMARY
Questionnaire layout.

Criteria for a good questionnaire

The quality of a questionnaire or test is defined on the basis of its reliability and validity (Cronbach, 1990; Oppenheim, 1992). Questionnaires depend on estimates or self-description rather than direct measurement. As a result one cannot be absolutely certain that the test instrument measures accurately what it intends to measure. However, there are techniques to assess whether the questionnaire produces reliable and valid results.

Reliability

Reliability describes the stability and consistency of the data. It is established by checking the consistency of data over time (repeated measures), or over slightly different but equivalent measures (more than one item or scale). There are several different ways to estimate the reliability of a test: test–retest, parallel forms, internal consistency, and inter-rater agreement.

Test–retest reliability

The most straightforward technique for assessing the reliability of a test is to administer the test twice to the same respondents, after a time interval of, say, two weeks. This would yield two measures for each person: a score on the first and on the second occasion. A correlation coefficient is calculated from these data which can vary between 0 and 1 (a negative correlation hardly occurs, except by accident). The higher the correlation between the two measures, the higher the reliability of the instrument. If the correlation equals 1 there is perfect reliability: the respondent obtained exactly the same score on both occasions. However, this rarely happens in psychological research. Generally, if the reliability lies within the range of 0.7 to 0.8 we can say that the reliability of our questionnaire is satisfactory, a correlation within the range of 0.8 to 0.9 is considered good, and above 0.9 as very good.

The test–retest method is inappropriate for assessing the reliability of knowledge tests, where skills learned on the first administration will transfer to the second. Differences in motivation and memory might also influence results. For example, the respondents might be bored, annoyed, less anxious, or might remember the questions. These difficulties can be overcome by timing the second administration very carefully.

Parallel forms

For this type of reliability assessment you will have to develop two versions of the same test which are linked in a systematic manner—each intending to measure the same construct. For example the arithmetic task: "Add 2+7" in the first version can be substituted for the task: "Add 3+6" in the alternative version. Each person is given both versions of the test and a correlation coefficient is calculated between the two responses. Although the use of parallel forms is the best method for estimating reliability, it is very rarely used because of its requirement to develop two different but equivalent tests, which means twice the amount of effort and time.

Internal consistency

A more practical method for estimating reliability is based on the comparison of each part of the test with all other parts. Internal consistency is an estimate of how consistent each part of the test is with all other parts. This can be done in two ways: either divide the test into two subcomponents (split-half reliability), or compare each item with each of the other items (Cronbach's alpha) (for details see Cronbach, 1990, Chapter 6).

Split-half reliability.　Divide the test into two parts, either by using odd and even items, or contrasting the first with the second half of the test. The two sets of scores are then correlated, and the reliability coefficient for the whole test is estimated. The major problem with this form of reliability assessment is to divide the test into two comparable parts, especially in situations where two different concepts such as reading ability and language skills are measured.

Cronbach's alpha.　This method provides an estimate of the correlation of each item of the test with all other items; the inter-item correlations. The alpha is related to the average of all the inter-item correlations. The higher the correlations between the items, the greater the internal consistency. This comparison assumes that all the items are indicators of a common characteristic.

Inter-rater consistency

This form of reliability assessment is used when responses are not scored objectively, i.e. according to pre-fixed response alternatives, but subjectively. This can be the case with open-ended questions, where there are no response options formulated, but each response has to be coded and classified. Generally this is done by two raters and each of them gives their own classifications. Then the level of agreement or disagreement between the two raters is calculated.

Validity

The notion of validity refers to the extent of matching, congruence, or "goodness of fit" between the questionnaire and the concept it is assumed to measure. Do the questions truly reflect what the concept means? Are you actually measuring what you intend to measure with this questionnaire?

The question of *what* tests measure is not entirely unrelated to *how* they measure. In a simple direct measurement such as reaction time measures—reaction time is measured. Yet, if the aim of a test is to measure a theoretical construct such as personality, ability, or aptitude, how can you know that a given test measures, for example, mechanical ability or language-learning aptitude? The question of what tests measure is known as the validity question. We can differentiate the following different types of validity assessment:

Face validity.　This is assessed by having experts review the contents of a test to see if they seem appropriate "on the face of it". This is a rather fuzzy procedure for validating a test, because of its inherent subjectivity. It is typically used only during the initial phase of test construction.

Content validity. This examines the extent to which the test specification under which the test was constructed reflects the particular purpose for which the test is being developed. One has to check whether all major aspects of a particular phenomenon are covered by the test items, and in the correct proportion. Then each item has to be reviewed to determine whether it is appropriate to the test, and to assess the overall cohesiveness of the test items. For example, a test of mathematical abilities should not phrase the items in such a way that verbal abilities are critical for the person taking the test to understand what is being asked. Furthermore, the contents should be balanced so that all tested aspects are represented appropriately, and the test should not be overloaded with, say, multiplication items to the neglect of addition items. Establishing content validity is largely a subjective operation and relies, like the establishing of face validity, on expert opinion.

Predictive validity. Another, more practical form of validation is predictive validity. This establishes the extent to which the scores on a test are predictive of actual performance. It is perhaps best understood in terms of aptitude testing, in which the aim is to predict from the test score how well the respondent will do in, for example, a job for which s/he has not yet received specific training.

For example, a test designed to measure clerical skill will have high predictive validity if it predicts who will and will not succeed in clerical jobs. Thus predictive validity is represented as a correlation between the test score and a score of the degree of success in the selected field.

Concurrent validity. This describes the correlation of a new test with existing tests that have proved successful at measuring the same construct. For example, a new intelligence test ought to correlate with existing intelligence tests. This is, however, not a satisfactory criterion on its own as the old and the new test may well both correlate and yet neither may be measuring intelligence. If, on the other hand, old and new tests fail to correlate, something must be very seriously wrong.

Construct validity. This consists of any empirical data that supports the claim that a given operational definition measures a certain concept. Such evidence may be derived from a wide variety of sources—and therefore, construct validation is not associated with a particular approach or type of evidence. No single study or piece of evidence is sufficient; construct validity of a concept is only as compelling as the amount and diversity of evidence supporting it.

SUMMARY
How to evaluate the quality of a questionnaire.

- Questionnaires are judged on the basis of their reliability and validity.
- Reliability refers to the stability and consistency of your data over time, across individuals, and across situations. It is assessed through:
  - test–retests;
  - parallel forms;
  - internal consistency estimates;
  - inter-rater consistency.
- Validity concerns the question of what the questionnaire actually measures: how well does the questionnaire measure what it is intended to measure? The major types of validity assessment are:
  - face validity;
  - content validity;
  - predictive validity;
  - concurrent validity;
  - construct validity.

Exercises

1. Please improve the following questions:
   i. Do you usually get up early?
   Yes [ ] No [ ]
   ii. Do you approve or disapprove of people who go to football matches?
   Yes [ ] No [ ]
2. You have designed a questionnaire where it is very important that every respondent answers each question in the right sequence. What mode of data collection would you choose and why?
3. You want to investigate risk-taking behaviour among teenagers. After researching the relevant literature, you cannot find a questionnaire that you think is appropriate, and you decide to develop your own instrument. You remember that your questionnaire should be reliable and valid. How would you go about designing your project?

References

Bourque, L.B, & Fiedler, E.P. (1995). *How to conduct self-administered and mail surveys.* London: Sage.

Converse, J.M., & Presser, S. (1986). *Survey questions: handcrafting the standardised questionnaire.* Beverly Hills, CA: Sage.

Cronbach, L. (1990). *Essentials of psychological testing.* (5th edn.). New York: Harper Collins.

De Lamater, J. (1982). Response effects of question content. In W. Dijkstra & J. van der Zouwen. *Response behaviour and the survey interview.* London: Academic Press.

Dillman, D.A. (1978). *Mail and telephone surveys.* New York: Wiley.

Fink, A. (1995). *How to ask survey questions.* London: Sage.

Fowler, F. (1995). *Improving survey questions: Design and evaluation.* London: Sage.

Groves, R. (1989). *Survey errors and survey costs.* New York: Wiley.

Jowell, R., Brook, L., Dowds, L., & Ahrendt, D. (1993). *British social attitudes: The 10th report.* London: SCPR.

Kline, P. (1986). *Handbook of test construction.* London: Methuen.

Moser, C.A., & Kalton, G. (1971). *Survey methods in social investigation.* Aldershot, UK: Gower.

Oppenheim, A.N. (1992). *Questionnaire design, interviewing, and attitude measurement.* (New Edition). London: Pinter Publishers.

Payne, S.L. (1980). *The art of asking questions.* Princeton, NJ: Princeton University Press.

Robson, C. (1993). *Real world research.* Oxford: Blackwell.

Rosenthal, R. (1976). *Experimenter effects in behavioral research* (Enlarged Edition). New York: Irvington.

Schuman, H., & Presser, S. (1981). *Question and answers in attitude surveys: Experiments on question form, wording, and context.* New York: Academic Press.

Sudman, S., & Bradburn, N.M (1982). *Asking questions: A practical guide to questionnaire design.* San Francisco: Jossey Bass.

Tourangeau, R. (1984). Cognitive science and survey methods. In T. Jabine, M. Straf, J. Tanur, & R. Tourangeau (1984). *Cognitive aspects of survey methodology: Building a bridge between disciplines.* Washington: National Academy Press.

People, materials, and situations 6

Daniel B. Wright

Aims

The aim of this chapter is to describe how methods fit into a more general way of viewing psychological research. In particular, the ways of gathering participants for studies, deciding on the materials, and devising the situations are discussed. Many of these different facets of psychological research are related. Understanding these will be useful when you are reading about studies, or constructing your own studies, particularly when the design is more complex than the ones that are discussed in this book. The framework presented helps to identify the types of inferences that can be made within both psychological research and more generally within any scientific endeavour. This is a rather lofty claim, and in places some of the discussion verges on the abstract. However, various examples will be used to try to clarify these conceptual issues. Some practical advice, which should be useful when you conduct your own projects, will also be given.

Let us begin with the basic tools of psychological research. First, and most important, are humans. There are some exceptions, like computer simulations, animal studies, and some organisational research, where researchers do not examine individual people, but most do explore the behaviour and cognitions of individuals. For ethical reasons, some research cannot use humans, but the norm is to use them. In the next section the way in which people become the objects of study in psychological research is discussed in more detail.

Collecting (or sampling) people is obviously not the same as doing research. Something has to be done with them. This is the main thrust of this book: the materials must be devised in such a way that when used the researcher has a hope of expanding the horizons of psychology (albeit usually in small steps). Devising appropriate instruments to measure whichever aspects are under investigation is difficult; similar problems are faced in all the sciences. While physicists have spent astronomical amounts of money to measure unobservable theorised entities like electrons, quarks, and neutrinos, psychologists have spent much of the last hundred years trying to measure attitudes, cognitions, intelligence, personality types, and other equally unobservable entities. Cattell (1988, p.3), one of the major researchers of personality, elegantly describes the discipline's journey: "the ship of psychology has perhaps at last cleared the rocky coast of popular illusions and the peril of false landmarks and has set out, well provisioned with new methodological resources, on the true bearings for the first stage of its ultimate voyage".

The final requirement for a psychological study is a place to conduct it. This sounds trivial, but it can be extremely important. From a practical standpoint, you would not want to measure someone's cognitive ability on the Friday late night train from London to Bedford to assess the person's normal functioning, nor would you want to assess a person's temperament with young offspring awaiting dinner. Social psychologists have shown how cognitions, behaviours, and measures of personality all vary according to the situation. The psychological laboratory, in its many guises, is a particularly peculiar situation. It shares some norms with more commonplace situations, but not others. Not only is it necessary to understand the peculiarities of the situations in which psychological research is conducted, but it is necessary to understand how inferences about human behaviours and cognitions in general can be made from these situations.

To summarise, people, in a situation, perform tasks usually with some materials. This is a framework for psychology research. More generally, this framework can operate for any scientific endeavour. Sometimes the importance of the materials, people, or situation is less obvious or critical, but they can always be identified. There is much discussion of stellar astronomy in the media, so this serves as a good example for comparison. Stars are our equivalent of humans. Astronomers' measurement devices are usually telescopes sensitive to a selected range of electromagnetic frequencies. The situation is that most telescopes are on Earth. Not only does the atmosphere present measurement problems, but astronomers view the universe only from this particular perch (or near it). With the exception of a few very bright objects, only stars within our region can be observed. It is very questionable how contemporary knowledge of the structure of the universe (and even its matter) in our own observable region generalises to other parts of the universe. Psychologists face similar problems deciding whether theories and findings generalise beyond the laboratory settings and sample in which they are explored. Fortunately, psychologists are not as constrained as astronomers in constructing and sampling materials and situations. Much psychological research is done with different populations, instruments and situations.

To recap some of the earlier discussion, the goal of scientific research is to evaluate and to construct relationships. These relationships can be either causal or associative. The relationships can be about people, materials, and/or situations. For experiments, psychologists look to see whether the manipulation caused a difference. If the difference between the conditions is large enough (statistical tests are used to determine how much is "enough"), then an effect can be attributed to the manipulation. For quasi-experiments, if the difference on some measure between the groups is large enough, then it is possible to conclude that the populations from which these groups were sampled differ on the measure (providing the same sampling procedures were used). There are, as discussed in earlier chapters, numerous assumptions that have to be made for these inferences to be valid, but this basic framework will suffice for present purposes.

"Make £5 by taking part in a psychology study": Recruiting participants

The interior decoration of psychology departments is done on an ad hoc basis, but the departments share a remarkable commonality. Toward the beginning of each year bulletin boards contain a few notes about joining clubs, renting spare rooms, and cheap prices for yesterday's computers. After the first few weeks of term, new notices go up asking for volunteer subjects saying it only takes ten minutes. You remember these notices; they attract the "good of science" volunteers. A few weeks later, because these good hearted volunteers are a scarce resource, the notices start offering either credits for your courses or monetary payment.

An interesting application of supply and demand economics occurs throughout the year. Supply goes down; many students are sick of taking part in psychology studies. Demand goes up; numerous students and staff members need to meet end of year/term deadlines for their research. Result: the prices go up and the notices get better (cartoons are even added to some of the notices!). The professional participants emerge who take part in all the studies thereby reaping the financial benefits of supply-side economics. While these people are still thanked in the same gracious manner as the "good of science" volunteers, their motives are different.

This lesson in basic economic theory should seem at odds with something told to you in your statistics courses (if you have had one) and in previous discussions in this book. One of the main assumptions of most statistical tests is that subjects are drawn at random from the population of interest. As any economist will tell you, the type of person who buys when prices are high is different from the type that buys when prices are low. Similarly, there is no reason to believe that "good of science" volunteers are the same type as the professional volunteers. Further, it is doubtful whether either of these could constitute a random sample of the population of interest. Random does not mean haphazard. With a random sampling process, "every possible sample has the same probability of being chosen" (Wright, 1997b, p.9). This definition of random is very different from the definition in many English dictionaries which alludes to a process without aim or method, and being done unconsciously. Random, in its statistical sense, has very specific aims and methods. The question is, how can researchers get away with using non-random sampling?

The answer is a little complicated by the fact that research often slips through the review process and gets published when the sampling method is not adequate for the inferences made. However, there are many times when the "please help" notices are legitimate, optimal, and even the only viable method. When you read other people's research, you should consider whether their sampling methods are adequate for their inferences. Do not assume that, because something is published, it is without fault.

There are several reasons why researchers continue to use easily attainable samples. Most obvious is the fact that they are easily attainable. This is a valuable reason and should not be downplayed. It means that time and effort can be used to collect more participants or used for other aspects of the research (or for essays, revising, having a life, etc.). Another reason often given is that these participants are highly educated and it is believed that they have the unique ability to understand even convoluted instructions. Given the willingness and the capability of the general population to answer complex questions in surveys, this reason does not seem justified. Anyway, convoluted questions should generally be avoided even with sophisticated audiences. A better reason is that the people usually recruited to psychology studies are relatively *homogeneous*. This means that while there are differences among them, they have more in common than you would expect from a random sample of the whole population. The most obvious commonality is education level (and sometimes course of study), but students also tend to be of similar age and to a lesser extent come from similar socio-economic backgrounds.

If doing a between-subjects experiment, the test statistic is a measure of the difference between the groups on the outcome measure divided by some measure of within-group variation. If the sample from which the groups are randomly allocated is homogeneous, then this within-group variation is likely to be smaller and therefore if a difference is present, it is more likely to be detected with a homogeneous sample. In statistical terminology, the *power* is increased. This increase in power can be attained with any homogeneous sample, not just university students. As discussed in the next section, in some situations it is sometimes easier to get non-students to take part in research.

With correlational designs, we are required to have a sample that is heterogeneous on the variable of interest.[1] Consider doing a study to see if there are age differences on some problem-solving tasks. If a student sample was used then it is likely that the age distribution would not be adequate to examine hypotheses about age differences. In this case you would want to make sure that there were lots of young and lots of older people. We would also want to make sure that there were no large differences in the way you sampled these groups. For example, you would want to be very cautious about sampling adolescents from a local park and adults from a large business in the city. The reason is that this difference in sampling frames—parks versus large businesses—may create a difference that could be confused with an age difference.

Some hints on gathering participants

The biggest fear that most students, about to embark on a research project, face is how to get people to take part. Going up to people and pleading for their help can seem like a belittling experience. Many potential participants have a different view. They are interested in taking part in the study and find it a welcome break from their normal routine. The trick is finding people who look as if they would like a break from their current activity.

Consider what many survey interviewers have to do. They knock on a stranger's door and ask if they can ask them 45 minutes of questions about soap powder and other equally riveting topics. And they get up to about an 80% response rate usually with no payment. The interviewers are welcomed into people's homes, often offered tea and biscuits, and the respondents are genuinely grateful. For most people, taking part in a survey or an experiment is a rare and atypical enough experience for the volunteer to talk gleefully about it for weeks.

You should, in general, sample from places where people have time to take part and are likely to be helpful. Below is a list of possible places with some of their characteristics. Many of these will be particularly good for some projects, but not for others. For example, if using a medical waiting room, the questions should be sensitive to the fact that some of the people are likely to be distraught.

Airports	People who have free time before boarding.
Launderettes	Small numbers of people with time to spare.
Train/bus stations	Despite the best efforts of privatisation, usually only quick studies can be done. Also, if there are long delays, people may be irritated.
Doctors'/dentists' waiting rooms	People may be ill and are unlikely to be in a gleeful mood.
Take-aways	Small numbers and usually just a short time.
Hair stylists	Small numbers and often not much space.
Cafeterias	People are often relaxing over coffee. A polite/pushy approach can recruit many participants fairly quickly.
On buses/trains	A fairly representative sample with people having time to spare.
Psychology lectures	Students may know the hypotheses. Also, they may ask you to take part in their studies.

For all the locations listed, you would be going up to people without having their names. When collecting a sample, it is often helpful to have lists of named people. Lists are useful in calculating the proportion of people who refuse to take part. You can also go back to people who initially refuse to ask for their assistance again and chase up people who were not available the first time you tried to contact them. The big survey and market research companies use lists that cover most of the country, like the phone books and/or the electoral register. Other lists include classroom registers (university/school), room lists (dorms and office blocks), and club lists. All these lists have their faults. For example, the electoral register will not include many people who did not register with the hope of avoiding taxes (so-called "poll taxes") and will include some people several times (which is legal in the UK, although you can only vote in one place), and the telephone book will under-represent single women who for safety reasons choose to be ex-directory.

- If doing an experiment, the group that you split into conditions should be as homogeneous as possible.
- If looking for differences based on characteristics of the sample, make sure the sample varies adequately on that characteristic.
- Recruit people at times when, and in places where, they will welcome a diversion.
- Ask people politely, but be direct.

SUMMARY
Participants in psychological research: some rules worth bearing in mind.

Materials and hypotheses

The last section focused on how to find people to study. Here, the materials are discussed. Now, much of this book is about constructing materials and describing where to find existing materials. Rather than attempting to condense a review of this into a single section, there will be a brief recap about how the choice of materials affects the type of conclusions that you would be able to make. Many of the issues are similar to the choice of participants. You want the set of materials that you use in your study to be in some way representative of a larger set of possible materials. For example, if you were comparing memory for nouns with memory for verbs, you would want the nouns and verbs you use in your study to reflect in some way the nouns and verbs used in normal English.

Consider another example. Suppose that you were interested in the relationship between the emotion induced by an event and the clarity of recollection of the event. There are two relationships in which you might be interested. The first is whether emotional events produce

Case study research

There is another type of research that is often discussed in clinical psychology, but is also used in other branches of psychology—case studies. Usually when people use the phrase "case study" they are describing a single person, but as will be discussed in later sections, the more common case study in psychology is where a single material or a single situation is used. Often case study research is downgraded because of the emphasis placed on attaining large samples for most purposes. This downgrading is sometimes justified. Some case studies are not done properly and offer little to our scientific knowledge. On the other hand, some case studies are done extremely well and the history of psychology abounds with case studies that have questioned existing psychological theories, and have pushed forward our knowledge of human psychology (for example, Ebbinghaus's research on his own memory, Luria's work on the mnemonist, subject S, and the clinical cases of Phineas Gage and HM).

To conduct successful case study research it is necessary to treat the individual person as the population of interest and perform the research within this population. Several tasks, different situations and many time periods should be sampled. Case studies serve a vital role with respect to falsification in the scientific process. Accordingly, an hypothesis is proposed and scientists try to observe some particular instance where it does not hold. Finding a single discrepant case means that the theory does not, in general, hold. This is why case study methods can be extremely useful in disciplines like psychology, which often use falsification as a scientific method.

clearer memories than other events. To explore these you would probably want to gather a large number of events from people's lives, have them rate some measure(s) of the emotiveness of the event, and then later see if there is an association between emotion and memory clarity.

This has been done. For example, Brewer (1988) gave participants an alarm that was programmed to "beep" at random intervals. When the alarm "beeped", participants were supposed to write down what they were doing and various aspects about it. Using this alarm defined the materials that were later to be remembered; the events. Brewer found that emotion and memory accuracy were positively related.

Brewer (1988) discusses how his data cannot establish a causal relation. It could be, for example, that the distinctiveness of an event leads to raised emotions and also leads to improved memory. The correlation may be spurious rather than causal (Simon, 1954). There are several conditions necessary for causal attributions to be made. Most important for present concerns is that the materials should be identical except for the particular characteristic to which you wish to attribute causality. In Brewer's study, the emotional events were likely to be different in many ways besides the emotion they evoked, compared with the non-emotional events.

In order to make causal statements there should be two (or more) events that are exactly the same except that one is emotional and the other is not. This allows us to examine the hypotheses of interest. The hypothesis that is usually tested, the null hypothesis (H_0), is that emotion does not alter memory performance, all other things being equal, in all circumstances. If this hypothesis is rejected, then we can accept that in some circumstances emotion alters memory performance. This is often called the alternative hypothesis (H_1).

Consider a study by Christianson and colleagues (1991). They had participants watch either a neutral slide sequence or an emotional slide sequence. The sequences showed a mother and her son leaving a house and walking down the street. In the neutral sequence the pair walked past a car and the mother dropped the boy off at school before returning home. In the emotional sequence the boy was shown on the hood of the car bleeding profusely with "one of his eyeballs … hanging out" (Christianson et al., 1991, p.696) and then being treated in a hospital emergency room. People in the emotional condition had better memory of central details.

The question is whether the experimental manipulation (the eyeball slide) changed more than just the emotion level of the sequence; are all other things equal? When viewing an emotional sequence, like the one used by Christianson et al., other beliefs about the story are likely to change. For example, seeing a child's eyeball "hanging out" is likely to increased the perceived importance of the event, and most studies of this type also find that importance and memory clarity are positively related. It is difficult to isolate many psychological variables. The researcher must identify the actual variable being described. In this case, researchers have to recognise that the introduction of the emotional slides may have caused the increase in memory, but that it may have caused other changes which couid also have affected memory.

Consider an example from Cahill et al. (1994) involving a placebo. Placebos are necessary because when people take a pill, they often believe that it will have some effect and this belief often produces an effect. This is known as a placebo effect. In order to isolate the chemical under investigation beyond these psychological effects, two pills that are exactly the same, except that one has the chemical under investigation, are administered. Within the same research genre as Christianson et al., Cahill et al. (1994) had people watch either a neutral

Ecological validity

According to Cohen (1989, p.3), "ecological validity has become something of a catchword" in psychology. It is often used by people to say that their research is applicable in some way outside the confines of their research laboratory. This can help funding prospects. It is, however, too vague a definition and some of the research going under this broad term (sometimes called "everyday cognition") has been justly criticised (see Banaji & Crowder, 1989). "Ecological" literally means the study of objects or people in relation to others and their surroundings. This is also not well defined; what are a person's "surroundings"?

Because of the variety of uses of this phrase, it is impossible to come up with a definition with which everyone will be happy, but it is worth trying. Ecological materials are those that are encountered in our normal daily lives and/or those for which people have developed to process both as individuals during their lifetimes and as a species throughout evolution. Similarly for situations, ecologically valid situations are those within which we have learned to process information. This classification is discussed in more detail in Wright (1997a).

slide passage or an emotional one. The difference was whether the slide sequence was described as a child being badly injured in a car crash (different slides from Christianson et al., though similar plots) or as a child visiting his father who works in a hospital. For this variable, Cahill and his colleagues needed to address the same concerns as just described (see Cahill & McGaugh, 1995, for discussion). They also had a second variable: half of the sample took a placebo and half had a drug that inhibits some of the pathways believed to be used for memory of emotional events. The placebo was necessary so that the effect of the drug (propranolol hydrochloride for those interested) would not be confounded by participants realising that they had taken some kind of pill. Cahill et al. were able to demonstrate that the drug significantly impaired memory for the emotional sequence. Because the only difference between the two pills was the drug, they could attribute causality to the drug.

It is important to stress that the distinction between these forms of hypothesis can be applied not only to the materials used in psychology, but also to explorations of different samples of people and situations. Consider, for example, whether heavy people have a better sense of humour than light people (associative hypothesis). This is a very different hypothesis from the causal one: heaviness causes increased humour. The causal one would actually be very difficult to study directly. Techniques that might be employed include showing participants themselves in distorting mirrors, having them weigh themselves on misleading scales, feeding them a vast quantities of pizza, etc. Each of these would be testing some particular aspect of "heaviness".

Finally, the two rather gory examples of cognitive psychology were not chosen simply to satisfy the author's macabre sense of humour. What happens if memory for horrific car crashes is different from that for plane crashes, viewing crimes, earthquakes, childhood sexual abuse, war tragedies, assassinations, and other negative emotional events? Memory for emotional events is important for several reasons including memory issues in post-traumatic stress disorder cases and the reliance of many police investigations on eyewitness accounts. The point is that Christianson et al.'s (1991) and Cahill et al.'s (1994) research are case studies where the cases are particular sets of emotional materials. While with person case studies the researcher has to examine that person in detail and to make reference to people in general, here the researcher must examine the particular set of materials in detail, making reference to a larger set of emotion-evoking material.

SUMMARY

There are two types of relationships that psychologists study: associative and causal. While in some more complex designs these can be combined, for our purposes it is easiest to consider them separately.

Associative:
- used to explore how characteristics vary naturally;
- the materials should be chosen to be representative of the population of interest.

Causal:
- to examine how a manipulation of some type influences other things;
- the sets of materials should be identical except for the aspect about which you want to make causal attributions;
- are easiest to explore using experiments.

Situations for psychological research

A large number of psychologists have shown the importance of the situation in all aspects of human behaviour and thought. For example, most of you will behave quite differently in a classroom from in a pub. Countless other examples could be given. Most of this research has been done by physiological, social, and environmental psychologists. In cognitive psychology the situation has often been looked at as a purely methodological issue. In this section three different ways in which the situation can vary—physiological differences, social differences, and differences in the physical environment—are discussed. These three overlap in many ways. For example, different physical situations alter both the physiology of the person and the social situation. They are differentiated here for explanatory ease.

The physiological situation

"Physiological situation" can have several meanings. Here it is used to mean the transient physiological state of the person. This means how, physiologically, the person differs from other situations. Characteristics like blood pressure, sugar levels, feeling ill, etc., all vary and all affect certain cognitive tasks. After some examples, the way that normal practice in cognitive psychology operates will be explained.

What time of day would you like to take an exam? Some people are "morning" people; some are not. In general, most people are fairly groggy early in the morning, particularly before those first drops of caffeine glide down their throats. Studying time of day effects is an active area in some branches of psychological research (sometimes called *chronopsychology*), but for most cognitive psychology experiments time of day differences are treated more as a methodological hindrance. Cognitive psychologists tend to recruit subjects in the late morning or in the afternoon when students are around. This is probably okay, as the times when people are poor performers (early morning and late evening) are usually avoided.

Time of day effects are based on both diurnal patterns (for example, Oakhill, 1988) and food/chemical intake (for example, Smith & Miles, 1986). Other physiological characteristics can also produce effects. As implied earlier, caffeine affects behaviour (and thought). Physiologically it is known that caffeine leads to further synaptic activation in some areas of the brain and that this leads to increased arousal.

Food, particularly food with a high sugar content, can also be helpful for many cognitive tasks. On the other hand, many other chemicals can negatively affect performance.

There is much research on all these physiological factors, demonstrating that each can affect cognition. The researchers usually use extremes in order to maximise the expected effect size and therefore increase the likelihood that they will observe an effect (in statistical terms, increasing the power). This is analogous to cognitive psychologists using extreme differences in their materials to maximise the power.

Cognitive psychologists usually try to avoid extreme situations. This has parallels to the reasons given for having a homogeneous sample of people with respect to some characteristic. By having the situations (or the samples) all similar, this decreases the expected individual differences and also increases the power. So, while in research designed to explore the effects of, for example, alcohol on performance, the researcher needs to make sure that the participants' alcohol levels differed, if the researcher was not interested in the effects of alcohol, then they would want everybody to be at approximately the same level (i.e. homogeneous with respect to alcohol). Usually this will mean sober, and you may have noticed that in the first section of this chapter, "pubs" were not included in the list of places to recruit people. In general, you should avoid extreme cases.

Mullin, Herrmann, and Searleman (1993) discuss how various physiological variables affect cognition. They have produced a questionnaire that could be handed out to participants which asks about stress, chemical and food intake, sleep, etc. This information could be useful for identifying any extreme cases that get into your sample. If you find some participants who, for example, were feeling very ill, then you could decide whether to drop them from the sample. It is worth noting that there are some advanced statistical procedures that could be used to "control" for some of these differences, but these procedures are beyond the scope of this book and are not always workable.

The social situation

You enter a room and sit down at a table. In front of you are 2000 sheets of paper. There are 224 simple addition problems on each. You are told to do the problems on the first sheet, and then to read the top card from another pile and follow the instructions. You solve the first 224 problems and then read the card: "Tear up the sheet of paper which you have just completed into a minimum of thirty-two pieces and go on to the next sheet of paper and continue working as you did before" (Orne, 1962, p.777). You do this and solve another 224 problems. The next card says the exact same thing. And the next. And the next, and so on. You continue for hours.

Before you consult the latest classification of obsessive/compulsive disorder or skim through the annals of Freud's work to discover what type of person would spend this long on such a task, consider that most of the people in the setting described continued for several hours. According to Orne (1962, p.777), "the subject will play his role and place himself under the control of the experimenter"; they will be compliant and not ask "why" they should perform seemingly meaningless tasks. This means they may try hard to get the "right" answers. In some areas of psychology this can create problems as people express "politically correct" beliefs that they do not really hold. It is difficult to measure true beliefs unless very innovative techniques are used (see, for example, Jones & Sigall, 1971). For most cognitive psychology research it is good to have people trying their hardest. In some studies participants are even offered extra money for "right" answers.

As such, cognitive psychologists are using a particular situation where optimally answering questions is encouraged. This makes it a relatively homogeneous situation. This sounds good, but it does present some limitations. For example, if we were interested in the strategies that people usually use for problem solving or memory retrieval or any other cognitive task, participants in a psychology experiment might try much harder than in other situations. The strategies and responses used in laboratory studies usually take more effort than in, for example, surveys (see Krosnick, 1991). There has been an increase in what is sometimes called *naturalistic cognition* in order to explore cognitive processes in their natural settings. There is much debate about the worth of this approach (see Banaji & Crowder, 1989, and replies in *American Psychologist*, 1991).

Outside the laboratory there are also various social forces that can influence behaviour. As with recruiting samples from pubs for reasons of toxicity, there are various guidelines worth mentioning. It is important to consider various aspects of the situation. For example, if you are using a train station to sample people, you should be aware that people will feel under time pressure and also that they will probably not give your study their undivided attention (in case there is an announcement about their train). Similarly, if you need somewhere quiet, choose somewhere that is quiet. Another popular "situation" is the telephone. There are various implicit social rules that people use when talking on the telephone and these will come into play. Also you cannot rely on showing the participants your materials.

Recently there has also been an increase in the number of people running experiments on computers. The materials may be the same as those used in pen-and-paper research, but they are presented on a computer and participants use the keyboard or mouse to register their responses. The computer is a situation with many social norms, as is evident by the hackers who get immersed in their cyber-worlds. Most people are not that accustomed to this medium or to the norms of these "experts". It is not clear how all the different types of people interact with computers. The three most practical pieces of advice that can be given about running studies on computer are (a) make everything absolutely clear because you may not be there to answer questions, (b) have the program foolproof so that accidentally hitting odd buttons will not destroy the program or the data, and (c) take advantage of what the computer does well (randomising conditions, recording response times, etc.).

The physical situation

Earlier in this section you were asked when you would like to take an exam. How about where? Imagine trying to do trigonometry with the parching sun of the Sahara charring your back. Okay, that is an extreme and as you are probably aware by now, while some psychologists purposefully create extreme conditions to test whether temperature affects cognitive performance (for example, Giesbrecht et al., 1993), cognitive psychologists avoid these extremes. Less extreme situations are also studied by environmental psychologists (a field also called *ergonomic* and *human factor* psychology). These psychologists study how various aspects of our environment are designed to help us work. An example is how the lighting in a room affects people on various cognitive tasks (Knez, 1995).

There are some additional characteristics about the impact of the situation that are particularly relevant to memory and are worth mentioning. They are also relevant to physiological situations. If you encode information in a particular situation, like being intoxicated on alcohol (Goodwin et al., 1969) or immersed in water (Godden & Baddeley, 1975), recall (though not recognition) can be better if you are put in that situation again. Besides being an important phenomenon for theories of memory, it means that for memory experiments it is very important to have knowledge of the situations.

This finding is also important outside psychology. For example, police officers are taught to use the *cognitive interview* when trying to get witnesses to remember details of a crime they have seen. One of the core principles of the cognitive interview is to have witnesses try to mentally reinstate themselves into the situation in which they encoded the crime (Fisher & Geiselman, 1992; Memon & Bull, 1991).

SUMMARY

The main conclusion from this section is that there are many different types of physiological, social and physical situations which people encounter in their daily lives. Three main points are worth reiterating:

- Differences among situations (physiological, social, and physical) can affect cognition.
- If you are interested in these effects, then make sure that your cases vary with respect to whichever situational characteristic is under investigation.
- If you are not interested in these effects, try to have all the participants in similar physiological, social, and physical situations.

These aspects are important for the design and analysis of data. For the discipline, it is important to see cognitive research advancing alongside the research that directly explores situational factors. This will help advance the discipline through, using Cattell's (1988, p.3) phrase, "its ultimate voyage".

Conclusion

In the introduction to this chapter, a framework for evaluating cognitive psychology was presented. Its core is that people perform tasks with some materials in a situation. This relatively simple-sounding three-part process is complicated by the fact that the types of people used in the sample, the types of materials used, and the types of situations used can all affect your results. In fact, most of the research in psychology concentrates on deviations on some aspect of these. The trick is trying to control for others, thereby isolating the effect of interest. The researcher must then argue that the results from the sample of people, of materials, and/or of situations used in the study, generalise to a much larger set.

Almost all of the points raised in this chapter apply to each of the three components of the research. For example, researchers can compare naturally occurring situations to observe whether there is an association. Strictly speaking this would not allow them to make causal statements about the link because other things may be different. Consider, for example, temperature and children's problem solving. There might be a direct effect of temperature on problem solving, but it might also be that in the warmer months children are not in school and this might affect their cognitive abilities. To make causal statements it would be necessary to conduct an experiment in which everything except for the temperature was the same. This is important to satisfy the "all other things being equal" condition of the causal hypotheses.

In the same way, if researchers wanted to compare aspects of their samples, for an associative hypothesis, they would need to sample people with different values on the variable. Thus, if they were comparing males' and females' ability on a cognitive task, they would sample several of each and see how the groups performed. This is an associative relationship. They could not make causal statements about this because all other aspects of these people, apart from their biological sex, are not the same. Because of this, many researchers have argued that gender, and other variables that we cannot even in principle manipulate, should not be regarded as having effects (see Holland, 1988, for details).

The framework presented in this chapter should help you to evaluate someone else's research as well as to design your own research. With respect to the people, the materials, and situations used in research, you should know which characteristics are attempted to be held constant (to make causal statements), which are being kept relatively homogeneous (to avoid extremes and therefore increase power), and which are either being purposefully varied (as in experiments) or allowed to naturally vary (in quasi-experiments). This

SUMMARY

A framework for psychological research was presented. Three critical aspects were identified:

- participants;
- materials;
- situations.

One of the core messages of this chapter is that each of these can be viewed in similar ways. Researchers usually focus on one of these and try to keep the others relatively consistent throughout the study.

will allow you to know both what types of inferences can be made from the study and also to which larger sets of people, materials, and situations the results are meant to apply.

Exercises

1. For Gardiner and Rowley, 1984 (reprinted in Chapter 9), write down the sample, materials, and situation used in the two studies. Say which aspects of each were controlled for, manipulated, and those sampled so that there was much similarity and those sampled for much dissimilarity.

2. Choose a paper with a single experiment from the recent literature (cognitive journals that often report single experiments include *Psychonomic Bulletin and Review, Quarterly Journal of Experimental Psychology, Applied Cognitive Psychology*, and *Memory*). Repeat exercise 1 for this study.

References

Banaji, M.R., & Crowder, R.G. (1989). The bankruptcy of everyday memory. *American Psychologist, 44*, 1185–1193.

Brewer, W.F. (1988). Memory for randomly sampled autobiographical events. In U. Neisser & E. Winograd (Eds.), *Remembering reconsidered: Ecological and traditional approaches to memory* (pp.21–90). Cambridge: Cambridge University Press.

Cahill, L., & McGaugh, J.L. (1995). A novel demonstration of enhanced memory associated with emotional arousal. *Consciousness and Cognition, 4*, 410–421.

Cahill, L., Prins, B., Weber, M., & McGaugh, J.L. (1994). β-adrenergic activation and memory for emotional events. *Nature, 371*, 702–704.

Cattell, R.B. (1988). Psychological theory and scientific method. In J.R. Nesselroade & R.B. Cattell (Eds.), *Handbook of multivariate experimental psychology (2nd Edn.)* (pp.3–20). London: Plenum Press.

Christianson, S.-Å., Loftus, E.F., Hoffman, H., & Loftus, G.R. (1991). Eye fixations and memory for emotional events. *Journal of Experimental Psychology: Learning, Memory and Cognition, 17*, 693–701.

Cohen, G. (1989). *Memory in the real world*. Hove: Lawrence Erlbaum Associates Ltd.

Cronbach, L.J. (1957). The two disciplines of scientific psychology. *American Psychologist, 12*, 671–684.

Fisher, R.P., & Geiselman, R.E. (1992). *Memory-enhancing techniques for investigative interviewing: The cognitive approach*. Illinois: Charles C. Thomas, Publishers.

Giesbrecht, G.G., Arnett, J.L., Vela, E., & Bristow, G.K. (1993). Effect of task complexity on mental performance during immersion hypothermia. *Aviation Space and Environmental Medicine, 64,* 206–211.

Godden, D., & Baddeley, A.D. (1975). Context-dependent memory in two natural environments: On land and under water. *British Journal of Psychology, 66,* 325–331.

Goodwin, D.W., Powell, B., Bremer, D., Hoine, H., & Stern, J. (1969). Alcohol and recall: State dependent effects in man. *Science, 163,* 1358.

Holland, P.W. (1988). Causal mechanism or causal effect: Which is best for statistical science? *Statistical Science, 3,* 186–188.

Jones, E.E., & Sigall, H. (1971). The bogus pipeline: A new paradigm for measuring affect and attitude. *Psychological Bulletin, 76,* 349–364.

Knez, I. (1995). Effects of indoor lighting on mood and cognition. *Journal of Environmental Psychology, 15,* 39–51.

Krosnick, J.A. (1991). Response strategies for coping with the cognitive demands of attitude measures in surveys. *Applied Cognitive Psychology, 5,* 213–236.

Memon, A., & Bull, R. (1991). The cognitive interview: Its origins, empirical support, evaluation and practical implications. *Journal of Community and Applied Social Psychology, 1,* 291–307.

Mullin, P.A., Herrmann, D.J., & Searleman, A. (1993). Forgotten variables in memory theory and research. *Memory, 1,* 43–64.

Oakhill, J. (1988). Effects of time of day on text memory and inference. In M.M. Gruneberg, P.E. Morris, & R.N. Sykes (Eds.), *Practical aspects of memory: Current research and issues. Vol. 2. Clinical and educational implications* (pp.465–470). London: Academic Press.

Orne, M.T. (1962). On the social psychology of the psychological experiment with particular reference to the demand characteristics and their implications. *American Psychologist, 17,* 776–783.

Simon, H.A. (1954). Spurious correlation: A causal interpretation. *Journal of the American Statistical Association, 49,* 467–479.

Smith, A.P., & Miles, C. (1986). Effects of lunch on cognitive vigilance tasks. *Ergonomics, 29,* 1251–1261.

Wright, D.B. (1997a). Methodologies for researching naturalistic memory. In D. Payne & F. Conrad (Eds.), *Intersections in basic and applied memory research* (pp.69–86). Hillsdale, NJ: Lawrence Erlbaum Associates, Inc.

Wright, D.B. (1997b). *Understanding statistics: Introduction to statistics for the social sciences*. London: Sage Publications.

Note

1. Heterogeneous is the opposite of homogeneous. *Hetero-* means different (in Latin), *homo-* means same, and *genus* refers to a group.

Ethics 7

Julia Nunn

Introduction

You may be wondering why a book such as this has a chapter on ethics. After all, science cannot tell us anything about ethics, because science is about understanding how the world works. It cannot prescribe or judge human behaviour. However carrying out scientific research can bring us into the realm of ethics and morality very quickly. For example, a researcher interested in determining the extent to which depression influences memory may find it hard to do so without sacrificing either the welfare of his/her participants or scientific rigour. One way of producing a tightly controlled laboratory experiment would be to induce depression in participants who had been randomly allocated to a "depressive" group. Velten (1968) devised a laboratory procedure for inducing depression which involved participants reading aloud statements associated with a target mood. It works: participants report feeling temporarily depressed and their performance on a number of tasks suffers.

Although such an experiment can be criticised on a number of grounds (is depression induced in the laboratory the same as other "real-world" depressions?) any potential scientific benefits in terms of knowledge and hence prevention/treatment of depression could, in any case, be (more than) offset by the disastrous effects on social and intellectual functioning that the induction of a depressed mood might bring about.

This is not to suggest that all, or even the majority of psychological research will pose such problems. Much research in this and other social sciences is free of ethical problems and therefore poses no threat to the people studied or to society at large. However ethical issues can crop up in what might seem, to the uninitiated, to be surprising places.

Aims

Behaving ethically is not as simple as it might seem! Thus the primary aim of this chapter is to sensitise the reader to some potential ethical pitfalls, which seems preferable to learning by trial and error.

What are ethics?

A good starting point for identifying an ethical problem might be to try and pin down what "ethics" are. Is an ethical problem the same as a moral dilemma, for instance? Essentially it is. Frankena (1973) defined *ethics* as a branch of philosophy that deals with thinking about morality, moral problems, and judgements of proper conduct. The term *ethical* denotes conformity to a code or set of principles. As you will see later on in the chapter, psychologists usually try to judge whether a piece of scientific research is ethical or not according to a set of guidelines, or principles, that aim to specify ethical behaviour within their discipline.

Useful though these guidelines are, referring to them can still leave a researcher unclear as to what course of action they should take. Why might this be so? Let's take a closer look at how an ethical or moral dilemma might occur.

How do ethical problems arise?

Ethical problems arise in research situations when two (or more) sets of values or interests are in conflict (Smith, 1975). Satisfying one set of interests can mean that the other set is neglected. This still might seem a fairly easy problem to solve: just pick the set of interests that will bring about the greatest good. However not only is it sometimes unclear what good will come from a particular course of action, it is also difficult to compare one kind of benefit with other kinds, because a "benefit" is hard to measure. In short, difficult choices need to be made for which there are still no clear-cut answers. For example, controlled trials for the testing of a new drug require some participants to be allocated to a group that receives a "placebo". The potential benefit of this kind of work is enormous: a cure for cancer, for instance. However the controlled trial may require that some participants are *not* given a drug that the researchers suspect may help them (the placebo group). Is it ethical to refuse to administer the drug to those people? The scientific benefit of properly testing a drug must be weighed up against the ethical importance of not withholding help from people. Measuring the relative benefits of scientific versus ethical values is hard. What would you do?

One goal of this chapter is to try to prevent ethical considerations from being viewed as obstacles to be overcome so that the "real" work of scientific research can begin. Hopefully, by considering some ethical dilemmas (such as the ones just quoted), the reader will start to view ethics as a challenging and dynamic topic within science, rather than a sermon about morality.

It is also worth pointing out, as Korchin and Cowan (1982) have noted, that the validity of scientific work and its ethical status are intertwined. Unethical practice can reduce the external validity of the research if it results in research methods that cannot be translated into practice. On the other hand, research that is poorly designed can reduce the ethical standing of the research, because the potential scientific benefits that can accrue are often minimal, and therefore less likely to offset possible risks to the participants. So good ethical practice makes for better science.

SUMMARY

By now you should:

- be aware of what an ethical problem is;
- appreciate how ethical problems can arise;
- understand how science and ethics are related;
- be viewing ethical dilemmas as a challenge!

The rise of ethical concerns in psychological research

In the past few decades, ethical issues in the social sciences have become a topic of growing concern as researchers try simultaneously to produce valid scientific work and protect the welfare of their participants. An index of this rising concern is the number of ethical guidelines that have sprung up in an attempt to codify ethical behaviour. But why has this concern only been expressed recently? In the 1960s discussions about the ethical implications of social science were rare, despite the fact that experiments involving deception, privacy invasion, and threats to confidentiality were accepted as a valid way of conducting such research. Kimmel (1988) suggests that the discussion of ethical practices at that time was taken as an indication that one had not yet outgrown a pre-scientific nature, bringing into the scientific domain issues that did not belong there. Hopefully very few researchers still hold this view!

An outline of some of the important developments that led to a change of viewpoint and, in turn, to a rise of ethical concerns in psychological research appears next.

One of the earliest influences was that of World War II. Psychologists were called on during this time to devise a number of testing programmes, including the intelligence testing of thousands of recruits. When the war ended, the demand for these kinds of tests in civilian settings, such as personnel, accelerated. This gave rise to questions about privacy, confidentiality, and the misuse of test results that may not have seemed pertinent to the war effort. Thus the call for a code of ethics seems to have come about at least in part as a result of the application of psychology. Diener and Crandall (1978) suggest that the emergence of applied psychology destroyed the notion that research was invariably ethical and value-free.

In the 1960s, behavioural scientists began to attend to ethical issues when debates about their methodology came to the fore. One such issue concerned deception, in part at least because at that time much social psychological research used deception as an integral part of the experimental design. Topics that were addressed using deception included attitudes (e.g. Festinger & Carlsmith, 1959), aggression (e.g. Berkowitz, 1962, 1969) and obedience (e.g. Milgram, 1963). The latter produced such a furore that it deserves further discussion. As Kimmel (1996) notes, the Milgram obedience project is often cited as the behavioural research most responsible for the growth of interest in ethical issues (e.g. Rosnow, 1981).

Milgram's obedience studies

Following Kimmel (1988), after a brief description of the research itself, an overview of the ethical debate will ensue.

Stanley Milgram's experiments involved an elaborate deception that led participants to believe that they were giving dangerous electric shocks to an innocent victim. Milgram recruited volunteers to take part in an experiment "on the effects of punishment on learning". Participants played the role of teachers who were given the task of teaching a list of words to learners. The latter were in fact aides of the experimenter. Participants were required to "punish" any mistakes the learner made by delivering increasingly strong electric shocks—in fact the learner didn't receive any shocks, but instead made deliberate mistakes and pretended to be in pain upon receipt of the "shocks". Underlying this rigmarole was the desire to observe the extent to which participants obeyed the authority of the experimenter. Despite the apparent agony of the "learners", participants were instructed to continue to administer increasingly painful shocks—and did so. The high degree of obedience observed under these conditions was unsettling, to say the least. Might ordinary people be capable of such cruelty under other circumstances?

Critical reactions to the obedience studies began to pour in almost as soon as the work was published. Not surprisingly, it was argued that inadequate measures were taken to protect the participants and that if the unethical nature of these experiments could not have been foreseen then they should at least have been stopped as soon as the stress on the participants became apparent (see Kelman, 1967).

Milgram (1963) responded to these complaints by asserting that adequate measures *were* taken to protect participants. These included the freedom to leave the experiment at any time, and a thorough debriefing at the end of the experiment, during which it was revealed that the apparent "victim" was in fact a colleague of the experimenter. Somewhat surprisingly, perhaps, the participants themselves later endorsed the experiments in a follow-up questionnaire, which Milgram interpreted as evidence that his participants had *not* suffered injurious effects.

Whether or not you agree with Milgram's points, the obedience studies and other leading cases that have not been discussed here added to the climate of increased ethical awareness within psychology. Moreover, at a broader, societal level, the civil rights movement and populism of the 1960s and 1970s exerted an influence on psychological research in the form of greater sensitivity to ethics (Korchin & Cowan, 1982).

Thus at a time when psychology as a discipline was suffering from growing pains, a re-evaluation of its ethics seemed appropriate. Trust in a discipline can be undermined in many ways; here was a clear-cut example of one way in which psychology had to clean up its act. Consequently a number of ethical guidelines have sprung up—e.g. those by the American Psychological Association (APA), and the British Psychological Society (BPS).

Ethical guidelines

In this section the APA guidelines receive particular emphasis because they are widely viewed as representing the most extensive and elaborate statement of ethics among those adopted by behavioural scientists.

The APA guidelines, first introduced in 1973, have undergone a number of revisions (1982, 1990, 1992). Although the organisation and precise content of different versions may differ, the basic ethical components do not change. The important ingredients for ethical conduct continue to be informed consent, cost–benefit assessments, protection from harm, and debriefing. The association has outlined 10 general principles governing the conduct of research with human participants, which are set out in the panel.

The APA's ethical principles in the conduct of research with human participants

A.   In planning a study, the investigator has the responsibility to make a careful evaluation of its ethical acceptability. To the extent that the weighing of scientific and human values suggests a compromise of any principle, the investigator incurs a correspondingly serious obligation to seek ethical advice and to observe stringent safeguards to protect the rights of human participants.

B.   Considering whether a participant in a planned study will be a "subject at risk" or a "subject at minimal risk", according to recognised standards, is of primary ethical concern to the investigator.

C.   The investigator always retains the responsibility for ensuring ethical practice in research. The investigator is also responsible for the ethical treatment of research participants by collaborators, assistants, students, and employees, all of whom, however, incur similar obligations.

D.   Except in minimal-risk research, the investigator establishes a clear and fair agreement with research participants, prior to their participation, that clarifies the obligations and responsibilities of each. The investigator has the obligation to honor all promises and commitments included in that agreement. The investigator informs the participants of all aspects of the research that might reasonably be expected to influence willingness to participate and explains all other aspects of the research about which the participants inquire. Failure to make full disclosure prior to obtaining informed consent requires additional safeguards to protect the welfare and dignity of the research participants. Research with children or with participants who have impairments that would limit understanding and/or communication requires special safeguarding procedures.

E.   Methodological requirements of a study may make the use of concealment or deception necessary. Before conducting such a study, the investigator has a special responsibility to 1) determine whether the use of such techniques is justified by the study's prospective scientific, educational, or applied value; 2) determine whether alternative procedures are available that do not use concealment or deception; and 3) ensure that

---

the participants are provided with sufficient explanation as soon as possible.

F.   The investigator respects the individual's freedom to decline to participate in or to withdraw from the research at any time. The obligation to protect this freedom requires careful thought and consideration when the investigator is in a position of authority or influence over the participant. Such positions of authority include, but are not limited to, situations in which research participation is required as part of employment or in which the participant is a student, client, or employee of the investigator.

G.   The investigator protects the participant from physical and mental discomfort, harm and danger that may arise from research procedures. If risks of such consequences exist, the investigator informs the participant of that fact. Research procedures likely to cause serious or lasting harm to a participant are not used unless the failure to use these procedures might expose the participant to risk of greater harm or unless the research has great potential benefit and fully informed and voluntary consent is obtained from each participant. The participant should be informed of procedures for contacting the investigator within a reasonable time period following participation should stress, potential harm, or related questions or concerns arise.

H.   After the data are collected, the investigator provides the participant with information about the nature of the study and attempts to remove any misconceptions that may have arisen. Where scientific or humane values justify delaying or withholding this information, the investigator incurs a special responsibility to monitor the research and to ensure that there are no damaging consequences for the participant.

I.   Where research procedures result in undesirable consequences for the individual participant, the investigator has the responsibility to detect and remove or correct these consequences, including long-term effects.

J.   Information obtained about a research participant during the course of an investigation is confidential unless agreed upon in advance. When the possibility exists that others may obtain access to such information, this possibility together with the plans for protecting confidentiality, is explained to the participant as part of the procedure for obtaining informed consent.

Source: American Psychological Association (1973). *Ethical principles in the conduct of research with human participants.* Washington, DC; American Psychological Association (1982). *Ethical principles in the conduct of research with human participants* (revised edition). Washington, DC.

Copyright © 1973 and 1982, APA. Reprinted with permission. (The APA cautions that the 1990 *Ethical principles of psychologists* are no longer current and that the guidelines and information provided in the 1973 and 1982 *Ethical principles in the conduct of research with human participants* are not enforceable as such by the APA Ethics code of 1992, but may be of educative value to psychologists, courts, and professional bodies.)

A separate set of guidelines for animal research exists; however, as this book is primarily concerned with practices relevant to cognitive psychology, they have been omitted.

As Kimmel (1996) has noted, few of the statements contained within the guidelines consist of absolute prohibitions. In most cases, the APA has clearly adopted a policy that emphasises the weighing of considerations that maximise benefits relative to costs (cost–benefit assessment). As a consequence, considerable thought and consideration on the part of the investigator is still required before ethical solutions may be reached.

Although it is probably fair to say that the guidelines for psychological research provide a reasonable framework within which researchers can analyse ethical issues, ethical dilemmas are not solved simply by reading such guidelines! The next section provides a commentary on some methodological issues provoked by the core components of ethical guidelines.

Translating ethical principles into valid research methods

Informed consent and deception

Informed consent means that the participants must be forewarned about those aspects of the research that may have detrimental effects. It is considered by many as the central norm governing the relationship between the investigator and the research participant. Although participants are not usually misled as to the *nature of the experiences* they will have during the experiment, they are however frequently misled as to the *true purpose* of the experiment. Both kinds of deception are typically carried out to control subject reactivity and are often harmless (for e.g. omitting to inform participants that a memory test might be given, in order to explore how well people recall information that they are not actively trying to remember). In the example just given, valid data could not be obtained if participants were fully informed of the purposes and procedures of the research. Studies have demonstrated that the informed consent procedure can seriously alter research results obtained in laboratory experiments, even without the disclosure of hypothesis-related information (e.g. Dill et al., 1982). However deception should never be treated lightly because the participant's consent is not fully informed as a consequence. Milgram's obedience studies (see earlier) highlight the dangers inherent in ignoring this important issue.

The APA believe that deception can be ethically justified from a cost–benefit perspective, if a particular study warrants it, and if certain safeguards such as debriefing and protection from harm are followed (see principles D and E). Others, however, believe that deception should be eliminated from research settings because its use violates a participant's basic right to informed consent (e.g. Baumrind, 1985). Clearly the jury is still out on this issue, and researchers must take great care in deciding whether the benefits of the deception procedure outweigh the risks to the participants.

Protection from harm and debriefing

In general, research should not harm the participants. However on occasion some people may freely consent to undergo unpleasantness or even pain for the greater benefit of humankind. Great care must be taken to ensure that no coercion, however subtle, takes place. In these situations a trade-off emerges between harm to the participants and potential gain at a societal level from the knowledge acquired.

In psychological research this harm is most likely to take the form of painful memories or embarrassment. One extreme example has already been discussed—Milgram's obedience studies. Participants should always have a way to contact the investigator after the research is over, because even apparently minimal-risk research may have unintended after-effects.

One way of avoiding such unintended effects is for the researcher to provide a thorough debriefing. This means that the investigator explains the purposes of the research (which may not have been apparent in studies employing deception), and describes clearly why any deception was necessary. It has also been suggested that the debriefing procedure entail an expression of regret on behalf of the researcher for having deceived the participant (Rosenthal & Rosnow, 1991).

In addition to the ethical functions of debriefing, two methodological functions may also exist. One concerns finding out whether the experimental manipulations were successful or not. If participants can reflect on the study and describe what they think about it, researchers may be able to identify whether the research situation was understood as intended and unearth previously unthought-of problems. However participants may view the debriefing procedure as a continuation of the experiment and therefore continue to adopt the subject role they assumed during the experiment.

A second methodological benefit of debriefing is that it may help to prevent participants telling other potential participants about the nature of the study. That is, part of the debriefing procedure can involve a request for secrecy. Explaining in some detail how certain benefits will be lost if the full procedure of the study is known in advance may well limit the extent to which relevant information is passed on. However it is unclear to what extent a pledge of secrecy actually limits the passage of information.

It has also been suggested, and pretty well accepted, that debriefing should fulfil an educational role in addition to those already discussed. This would mean that participants receive an educational benefit in return for taking part in the study. The education could take a number of forms, for example information about the psychological phenomenon under scrutiny, self-knowledge, and/or a better understanding of the scientific process.

Privacy and confidentiality

Privacy and confidentiality are two ethical issues that are crucial to social scientists, who, by the very nature of their research, frequently ask people to share with them their thoughts, attitudes, and experiences. Invasion of privacy and loss of confidentiality are special cases of harm. Privacy refers to the person's right not to provide information to the researcher, while confidentiality refers to the person's right (and the researcher's corresponding obligation) to withhold information from third parties.

In some sense all psychological research invades privacy, as otherwise no new information could ever come to light. However the sense in which it is meant here is bound up with the intrusiveness of research. People vary in the extent to which they mind disclosing intimate information about themselves: some aren't bothered, others have a strong need to maintain rigid control over what is known about them. Researchers need to be aware of each person's limits on disclosure and respect their right to withhold certain information.

Although no confidentiality guarantee can ever be absolute, as data must always to some extent be prone to theft, a great deal can be done to maximise available protection. The commonest means of protecting a research participant's identity is to code participants' identities and data separately. Adopting practices such as this also encourages participants to be more open, and thus yield better data, than if they fear freedom of information.

In an ideal situation the informed consent form should specify who will have access to the data and for how long. Participants' personal details should also be masked when writing scientific papers.

So far the principle of confidentiality probably seems quite straightforward, and unlikely to give rise to an ethical dilemma for a thoughtful researcher. However the principle of confidentiality can come into conflict with the principle of protection from harm. A good example is provided by Elmes et al. (1995). Participants in an experiment completed a clinical test designed to assess their current level of depression, but were assured that their answers would remain confidential. If a participant scored high on the test and was also receiving psychotherapy, the experiment terminated at that point (the investigators wanted to screen out people with depression from subsequent elements of the experiment). So far, so good. However an ethical dilemma arose when it was discovered that one of the participants scored very high on the depression test, and was not receiving any kind of treatment. Because the test was known as a reliable and valid predictor of serious, clinical depression, and the participants were college students, the principal investigator felt that it was necessary to tell the college counsellors that one of the students appeared to have very high levels of depression.

This case illustrates a common ethical dilemma. To stick to one ethical principle can necessitate violating another. To the investigator in question it seemed more important to make sure the student received help than to uphold their right to confidentiality. Someone else may have made a different decision. What would you have done?

SUMMARY

By now you should:

- be able to give an outline of some influences on the rise of ethical concerns within psychology;
- understand the general ethical principles contained within the APA guidelines;
- appreciate some of the methodological issues that arise from following ethical principles.

Exercises

1. *Case study*. Describe the ethical problems posed by the following example of psychological research. Under which circumstances, if any, might this project be acceptable? An experiment is proposed in which, in order to understand and ultimately cure severe anxiety, eight human subjects will be required to consent to a procedure that will induce a temporary but incapacitating level of anxiety. The researchers intend to report the results of the study in a scientific journal.

2. Read the Milgram article (Milgram, 1963). What precautions do you think Milgram should have taken *before* starting his research programme?

3. Find an example of a research study from your lectures or laboratory classes that you believe raises ethical issues. What exactly are those ethical issues? How could the experiment have been conducted differently in order to avoid them?

References

American Psychological Association (1973). *Ethical principles in the Conduct of Research with Human Participants*. Washington DC: APA.

American Psychological Association (1982). *Ethical principles in the conduct of research with human participants* (rev. edn.). Washington DC: APA.

American Psychological Association (1990). Ethical principles of psychologists. *American Psychologist, 45*, 390–395.

American Psychological Association (1992). Ethical principles of psychologists and code of conduct. *American Psychologist, 47*, 1597–1611.

Baumrind, D. (1985). Research using intentional deception: Ethical issues revisited. *American Psychologist, 40*, 165–174.

Berkowitz, L. (1962). *Aggression: A social psychological analysis*. New York: McGraw-Hill.

Berkowitz, L. (1969). The frustration–aggression hypothesis revisited. In L. Berkowitz (Ed.), *Roots of aggression*. New York: Atherton.

Diener, E., & Crandall, R. (1978). *Ethics in social and behavioral research*. Chicago: University of Chicago Press.

Dill, C.A., Gilden, E.R., Hill, P.C., & Hanselka L.L. (1982). Federal human subjects regulations: A methodological artifact? *Personality and Social Psychology Bulletin, 8*, 417–425.

Elmes, D.G., Kantowitz, B.H., & Roediger III, H.L. (1995). *Research methods in psychology* (5th edn.). St. Paul, MN: West Publishing Company.

Festinger, L., & Carlsmith, J.M. (1959). Cognitive consequences of forced compliance. *Journal of Abnormal and Social Psychology, 58,* 203–210.

Frankena, W.K. (1973). *Ethics* (2nd edn.). Englewood Cliffs, NJ: Prentice Hall.

Kelman, H.C. (1967). Human use of human subjects: The problem of deception in social psychological experiments. *Psychological Bulletin, 67,* 1–11.

Kimmel, A.J. (1988). *Ethics and values in applied social research.* Newbury Park, CA: Sage.

Kimmel, A.J. (1996). *Ethical issues in behavioural research.* Oxford: Blackwell.

Korchin, S.J., & Cowan, P. (1982). Ethical perspectives in clinical research. In P.C. Kendall & J.N. Butcher (Eds.), *Handbook of research methods in clinical psychology.* New York: Wiley.

Milgram, S. (1963). Behavioral study of obedience. *Journal of Abnormal and Social Psychology, 67,* 371–378.

Rosenthal, R., & Rosnow, R.L. (1991). *Essentials of behavioral research: Methods and data analysis* (2nd edn.). New York: McGraw Hill.

Rosnow, R.L. (1981). *Paradigms in transition: The methodology of social inquiry.* New York: Oxford University Press.

Smith, N.L. (1975). Some characteristics of moral problems in evaluation practice. *Evaluation and Program Planning, 8,* 5–11.

Velten, E.A. (1968). A laboratory task for the induction of mood states. *Behavioral Research and Therapy, 6,* 473–478.

Writing experimental reports 8

Zofia Kaminska

Aims

Most students enjoy doing experiments. In a recent survey the experimental laboratory course was voted the most popular course of the first year. But just as learning about experimental method is an essential part of training in psychology, so reporting experiments is an integral part of experimentation and research, and one of your course requirements will be to write reports on the experiments carried out. (If your course doesn't require this then there's something wrong with the course—you'll understand why when you've read the next section.) And some students find the task a little daunting.

"Are reports really necessary? We've understood the experiment, why bother to write about it?". "It's time-consuming". "It's confusing—I never know what to put in each section". "Why must it be in this special format? As long as it's clear what does it matter how it's presented?" These are just some of your frequent comments.

So the purpose of this chapter is to answer these *cris de coeur*, to explain why writing reports is important in general and valuable to you personally, and to help you through the early stages. By the end of the chapter you should be in a position to:

- appreciate the value of writing reports;
- know how to approach the task;
- be familiar with the format of a report;
- distinguish between the content of different sections;
- use an appropriate writing style.

Are reports really necessary?

Communication of findings is an inherent feature of scientific enquiry. Without such communication science could not progress; discoveries would go unknown and unnoticed. So one purpose of writing reports is to disseminate information. Another, and no less important one is to provide the potential for replication of the study, so that the reliability of the findings can be checked. Without this cycle of checks, challenges, corrections, and improvements, science would stand still.

Of course, it's quite likely that your experimental findings may not be new or newsworthy. This may be particularly true of early experiments, where the question posed may be relatively trivial—because, for instance, the experiment was planned simply to illustrate a particular methodological principle, or to demonstrate some well known psychological phenomenon. So, you may well ask, why bother writing a report? You've learned the principle, been introduced to the phenomenon.

But it's one thing to think you've understood something, quite another to demonstrate your understanding by being able to explain it clearly. In fact, it's often only when you come to write the report that you come to realise that you *don't* actually understand everything. So the third, rather composite function of the report is that it allows you to identify areas of your own misunderstanding, to clarify your ideas, and to *demonstrate* your understanding. Part of this clarification may come from wider reading, and it's those students who take the trouble to do some independent reading who gain the best degrees.

Finally, and again this is something of personal benefit, writing reports provides you with the opportunity to practise and improve, through feedback, your written communication skills. And although the practice may seem very specific to psychology, and not all of you will move on to do psychological research, the skills of conceptual analysis, organisation, and clear presentation of information will stand you in good stead whatever you go on to do in life. So the fourth function of report writing is that it provides a forum for learning a variety of skills.

SUMMARY Reasons for writing reports.	<ul><li>Communication of findings.</li><li>Provision of potential for replication, checking, and modification.</li><li>Clarification of ideas, increasing understanding.</li><li>Promoting wider reading.</li><li>Learning scientific written communication skills.</li></ul>

Format of the report

Your report will have to be written in a certain format, with specific sections, each with its own heading, describing different elements of the experiment. This format reflects scientific convention in reporting psychological research in journals (see Chapter 9), and the sooner you accept it and come to differentiate which elements of the experiment go into which section, the easier you'll make life for yourself.

The content of each section is discussed in some detail later in this chapter, but first let's take a look at the overall organisation of a report. Although there may be minor variations across different courses, the basic format is as follows:

Title. This should identify what the study is about in a single sentence.

Abstract. An outline summary of the experiment. A short paragraph summarising everything about the experiment—what was investigated, why, and how; the results, and interpretations of findings.

Introduction. The reason for conducting the study. Outline of the background to the experiment; description of relevant past research; a statement of the rationale and aim(s); a statement about the expected outcome (experimental hypothesis).

Method. A description of the study in sufficient conceptual detail to permit replication. The Method is divided into a number of sub-sections:

> **Design**. The basic framework of the experiment, the logical infrastructure of how the aim was to be met. An outline description of what was done, what was measured.
>
> **Materials/Apparatus**. Description of apparatus used; a description of materials—e.g. questionnaires, lists of words, pictures.
>
> **Participants**. The people (or other organisms) who took part in the study. Details of the number of participants, manner of sampling, personal details relevant to the experiment.
>
> **Procedure**. A detailed narrative step-by-step account (again to permit replication) of how testing of participants was carried out.

Results. A summary of the data collected. A verbal outline of the results, supported by a table of results (usually the mean values for each condition) and/or a graphical representation of data. This section includes a statement of how the data were analysed statistically, i.e. which statistical test(s) was used, and the outcome.

Discussion. A consideration of the results and their implications: General statement of findings. Interpretation of findings in relation to original aim/hypothesis(es). Consideration of results in relation to theoretical context of experiment (Introduction); consideration of theoretical and/or practical implications of findings; suggestions for further research.

Conclusion. Brief statement of outcome of study in relation to aim.

References. A list of all authors mentioned in the report, with full details of source information (usually journals or books).

Appendix/Appendices. Raw, uncollated data/verbatim instructions /details of actual stimulus materials/questionnaires and/or statistical computations.

The list of sections is quite lengthy and, in the abstract, may seem a little daunting. But in fact the main sections—from Introduction to Discussion, map very directly on to the different elements of the experiment that you carry out, which means that much of the information is actually organised for you. So when you're attending an experimental class, make a note of the different *types* of information that you acquire and where it will fit into the report.

Some general advice on writing your report

When to write a report

The sooner you write the report after completing the experiment, the better. Try for the same evening, or the following day, while everything is still fresh in your mind. Pieces of paper with scribbled data have an uncanny tendency to disappear, and you'll find that the apparently ample notes taken in class become quite enigmatic after a few days. Or, worse still, because everything seemed so clear at the time, you didn't bother to take notes …

How long will it take?

Those of you who cried "It's so time-consuming" are quite right. You must be prepared to spend a good few hours on the report at a minimum, sometimes even a whole day. There's no way you'll write a good report in, say, half an hour or even an hour. There's simply too much material in even the most straightforward experiment to produce an adequate account in such a short time. If you don't want to spend the time and effort that writing reports requires, then leave psychology and find some other courses to do.

When you start working on the report, DO prepare a rough draft first. It's most unlikely that you'll say what you want to say in the clearest, most informative and succinct way possible the first time round, and no one wants to mark a report that's bristling with crossings-out and omissions. In fact, if it's at all possible, try to produce the report (and, indeed, all written work) on a word-processor. This provides extra thinking time during composition, and makes adjustments to a draft very easy.

Who are you writing for?

It will help you to write at the appropriate level of explanatory detail if you can set up in your mind the audience for the report. No, this is NOT the person who'll be reading and marking the report. That person is likely to be familiar with the basic details of the experiment, from marking the first few reports if not from actually taking the class. Your aim is to write for an *imaginary* reader, a reader who knows NOTHING about the experiment, but who is sufficiently intelligent to understand all the information you care to present. You'll have to explain what was done, why it was done, what was found, and what the findings mean, with sufficient detail and clarity for your reader to understand everything completely, and—and this is of the utmost importance—be able to *replicate* the experiment exactly. This point of replicability is expanded in the Method section. But you can appreciate the level of detail and explanation at which you must write.

Writing style

Although some schools encourage very informal, direct, "first-person" reporting of investigations, where phrases such as "I heated the test-tube over a flame" are in order, this is not the convention in psychological reports. You should write your report in a more formal way, using the passive voice and an impersonal style. For instance, instead of saying "We selected words from a dictionary ..." use a phrase such as "Words were selected ...". Even where you're giving your own interpretation of something, avoid phrases such as "I think this is because ..." and replace them with phrases such as "A possible reason for this is that ..." Don't worry if this style of writing seems strange at first. You'll soon adjust to it and your writing will gain an air of sophistication.

With this more formal way of writing comes the fact that you should write words out in full—avoid collapsed forms of two words which are often used in colloquial speech where part of one word is omitted, and represented in written form by an apostrophe marking the omission. For example, write *"It is"*, not *"It's"*, *"have not"* not *"haven't"*, and so on.

Incidentally, in what sort of style is this chapter written? And why do you think that is?

Scientific writing: Substantiating your statements

One thing you'll quickly have to learn, both when writing reports and all psychology essays, is that it's not acceptable—because it's not scientific—to make unsubstantiated comments. Avoid giving your own opinion, however uncontroversial it may seem, e.g. *"I think most people get anxious during exams"*, or anecdotal evidence: *"Cheerful people like bright colours"*. Make sure that every claim you make is supported by acceptable evidence; that is, by findings from properly conducted research, and cite this research.

Citing other people's work

The way to refer to someone's work in the main body of the report is to mention them by name and to give the date or dates of when the particular research was published. A quick look at any journal article will show you how this is done.

For instance, *"Coltheart (1979) suggested that ..."*. Or you can mention the author less directly, e.g. *"According to the dual-route theory of reading (Coltheart, 1979) ..."*. If there is more than one publication by the same author, then separate the dates by commas in the text, e.g. *"van Orden (1987, 1991) ..."*. If you want to mention several publications in relation to the same topic, then separate the authors—plus dates—by a semi-colon. Thus: *"Coltheart, 1979; van Orden, 1987"*. When an article has more than two authors, cite the names of all the authors on the first occasion you mention the work, e.g. *"van Orden, Pennington, and Stone (1990)"*. On subsequent occasions you can use just the first author followed by *"et al."*. This is an abbreviation of the Latin *et alia*, meaning "and others". The fact that it is an abbreviation is signalled by the full stop after "al". For instance: *"van Orden et al. (1990) considered that ..."*. However, if there are only two authors, then it's not appropriate to put "et al." because there is only *one* other, and not "others". As it's not conventional to use the singular form of the Latin "other" (perhaps because it depends on a gender distinction) in scientific reports, you have to use both authors' names throughout.

The way to give full details of published work referred to in the text is described in the outline of the Reference section.

Plagiarism

Plagiarism is trying to pass off someone else's ideas or work as your own. It is considered a very serious offence, and many institutions impose severe penalties on students found committing plagiarism.

The written report you produce must be your own work. In one sense, you should have no difficulty in defining what is your own work—you must write it yourself and not copy from someone else. But the problem can be more subtle. The ideas and background research for the experiment were perhaps outlined for you, and you'll have done some background reading. You have to use that material in the report. But the ideas are not your own. What you have to learn to do is to present the material using *your own words*. However—and this may seem hard—even using your own words is often not enough. If it were, then you could in theory go through someone else's work re-phrasing every sentence so that the words would be your own. But this would still be plagiarism, because the general thought processes leading through that particular line of reasoning would not be yours.

So you must not only use your own words, but *create your own line of reasoning, your own structuring of arguments*. Again, try to recognise this as part of the learning process that writing a report affords. You are the one and only person to benefit from thinking about the issues and trying to relay them in the way that you've conceptualised them.

Many of you argue that something has been explained so well in whatever book or article you've read that you can't possibly say it any better. Even if this were the case (and it may not be, for in fact there are many examples of ambiguities and imprecise use of language in the literature),the point is that you *have to* say it in your own way. And please don't try to be clever, slipping in a copied sentence or paragraph to mingle with your own. It will stick out like a sore thumb, and while you may fool your imaginary reader, it will be more difficult to fool the real one. If you think it's worth trying, and happen to succeed, then the only person you really are fooling is yourself.

Abbreviations

While abbreviations used in colloquial speech are best avoided, other abbreviations are quite acceptable. One common one in psychological reports is the "et al." abbreviation. But it may be convenient to use others, specific to your particular experiment. If there's a term that you know you'll be using over and over again, then it's more efficient to produce an abbreviation for it, define it on the first occasion you use the term by giving the abbreviation in parentheses immediately after the term, and thereafter use just the abbreviation. For example, you could say something like "The original studies of reaction time (RT) may be attributed to ...", and, subsequently "Other studies on RT were carried out by ...". Experimental conditions, however, are best described with meaningful words, not abbreviations.

SUMMARY
General advice on writing your report.

- Write the report as soon as possible after completing the experiment.
- Allow a good length of time to produce the report—several hours minimum, and *write a rough draft first.*
- Write for an imaginary reader who knows nothing about the experiment.
- Use an impersonal reporting style.
- Substantiate all factual statements.
- Acknowledge other people's work by appropriate citation.
- Plagiarism. Don't even think about it.
- Make effective use of abbreviations.
- Use word-processing facilities if possible.

Producing the report

Although the different sections of the report have to appear in a particular sequence in the final version, there's no need to actually write the sections in this order. In fact, although the Abstract is basically the first section, it's best to leave it until last, when you've really mulled over the whole experiment and will be in a position to reduce it to a brief summary. So we'll leave the Abstract and the Title to the end, and go through all the other sections in sequence.

The Introduction section

The Introduction covers three basic conceptual elements:

- the motivation for the experiment, the reason why it was conceived;
- the background context, outlined in a review of relevant literature, from which the experimental question is derived;
- the aim(s) of the experiment with, often, a statement of the expected outcome.

These aspects are conceptually distinct but are not labelled as separate sub-sections, and there may be some interweaving of sections, particularly of the first two.

Structuring the Introduction

The simplest way to structure the Introduction is to start with the general background, and then narrow it down, leading ultimately into your particular research question and your experiment. Alternatively, start with an explicit question that the experiment addresses, and then step back into a context-setting description of the area. Whichever way you choose, move from a few general sentences to a description of more specific theories and research findings, perhaps a historical development of ideas, of arguments and counter-arguments that have been put forward in the literature, and then on to your own specific experimental question, showing how it derives from existing work.

For most experiments don't spring out of thin air. They stem from some unanswered question, some controversy, or some theoretical prediction based on previous research. Even when an experiment doesn't arise directly from existing theory, when it seems purely exploratory, it will usually be based on an observation that has in turn suggested some explanation, and the very fact that an explanation can be suggested indicates the existence of relevant information.

The main source of information for this aspect of the Introduction will be the introduction given in class or in a hand-out, though you'll need to supplement this with additional reading, either from specific references or from an introductory psychology text book. However, check that what you're including is relevant to the experiment. Remember that the literature survey isn't intended to be an all-embracing work of reference, but a selection of material from which you construct a story that leads up to and justifies doing your experiment. There's an art in weaving this Introductory story, so try to tell the most logical and interesting story you can. It may help you to describe the line of reasoning to someone who knows nothing about the experiment, to see how smoothly your story flows.

The final part of the Introduction should lead into a clear statement of the aim of the experiment, captured in a single sentence e.g.: "The aim of the experiment was to explore whether the orientation of a face affects face recognition". In addition, you may be able to make a *prediction* about the outcome of the experiment; that is, what you expect to happen. In the case of the example just given, the prediction might be that "There will be a difference in recognition as a function of orientation of the face". In some cases the prediction may be even more specific, specifying the direction of the difference, e.g. that "Upright faces will be recognised more easily than inverted faces".

This prediction is, in essence, the experimental hypothesis (H_1), but it is not explicitly labelled as such in scientific reports. However, some introductory courses may require you to do so, even contrasting it with the null hypothesis (H_0), particularly in the early stages, just to make sure that the question that will subsequently be tested statistically is clearly identified.

SUMMARY
Structure of the
Introduction
section.

- Outline the background context of the experiment: past theories, research findings, controversies.
- Describe the motivation for your experiment, how it derives from existing research, ending with a description of what the experiment will be about.
- Formal statement of the aim.
- Statement of the expected outcome.

The Method section

This section has to describe what happened in the experiment; what the plan of the experiment was, how it met the aim, how the plan was carried out, what data were collected.

Remember, there is one perfect guiding principle for this section: describe everything in such a way that anyone reading it could *replicate* the experiment exactly. Replication means precisely that: doing the same experiment again, using the same materials, the same type of subjects, the same method and procedure. When you've written the Method, try to get someone who's completely unfamiliar with the experiment to read it, and if they have *any* questions about how to carry out essentially the same experiment, then you haven't provided enough information.

Obviously, you need to exercise some common-sense in describing details of the Method. There'll be many things you could mention that are completely irrelevant, such as the colour of the walls of the room in which the experiment was conducted, or the day of the week on which testing took place. On the other hand, if the experiment was to do with some aspect of colour perception, or with productivity at work before and after a weekend break, then these facts may well be relevant.

Experimental design

True experiments.   It's best to start with a true experimental study, that is, one that seeks to examine the effect of manipulation of one variable, the independent variable (IV), on another variable—the measure of performance, the dependent variable (DV), as this provides the fullest example of experimental design. (For a discussion of the distinction between true experiments, quasi-experimental studies, and non-experimental studies, see Chapter 4.)

The design of the experiment is its blueprint, the abstract underlying structure. Don't worry if at first this seems mystifying —lots of people have trouble with it. Think of an experiment as a story: the design is the plot of the story. Consider all the novels you've read. There are actually surprisingly few plots, and the more abstract or generalised the level at which you envisage them, the fewer there are. The surface details, of course, can differ widely—names, characters, settings—but a common theme is detectable. The same is true of experiments. The psychological area, the question posed, the stimuli, and procedure will vary from experiment to experiment. But the number of different plots, of different designs, is relatively small. (See from Chapters 2, 3, and 4.)

So your task in this section of the report is to get across the plan of the experiment. It might help you to go through a sequence of decisions:

1. What was the independent variable (IV), the thing that was manipulated?

This must be presented at one level of abstractedness above that of the actual experimental conditions. Imagine an experiment that aims to test whether faces can be recognised as easily upside down as the right way up, with one experimental condition involving presentation of inverted faces; the other, faces the right way up. The independent variable, the thing that is being manipulated, the abstract umbrella concept above the actual experimental conditions of testing, is *the orientation of the faces*. Aim to reach this level of abstraction when describing the IV.

2. How many levels did the IV have?

How many different "settings" or values? The number of levels gives you the number of experimental conditions. In the previous example, the IV has two levels—upright or inverted orientation—generating two experimental conditions under which response measures are obtained. But the variable of orientation could, of course, have had more than two levels—upright, inverted, and horizontal, for example.

3. How was the IV operationalised?

How were the levels of the IV put into operation, into practice, made concrete? For instance, you could show participants photographs of faces, presenting them in normal orientation for the "Upright" condition, or turned upside down for the "Inverted" one. That would satisfy the design requirement of having those particular two levels of the IV, upright and inverted faces. But you *could* ask your participants in the "Inverted" condition to stand on their heads to view real faces. This would represent a different, but no less valid, way of operationalising the design.

In fact, asking participants to stand on their head for one of the conditions would introduce a confounding variable into the experiment, an additional difference between the conditions over and above that created by the manipulation of the IV and, as you know, the aim of a true experiment is to find the effect of changes in the IV, and ONLY the IV, on the dependent variable. So an alternative might be to ask the owners of real faces to stand on their heads to produce inverted face stimuli for viewing by upright participants in the "Inverted" condition. The possibilities are endless… But you can see that there are numerous ways in which you can achieve the theoretical requirement of a variation in face orientation; that is, ways in which the infrastructure of the experiment can be realised in practical, concrete terms; ways of putting surface details on the basic plot.

In slightly more advanced experiments you may have more than one IV. For instance, face recognition could be tested as a function of orientation and of the species of the face—human versus animal, for example. Don't panic. Just go through the same descriptive procedure for each IV in turn.

4. Type of manipulation.

Either now, or before the preceding point, say how the manipulation of the IV was carried in relation to the participants. Was it within-participant or was it between-participants? That is, was each participant tested in condition of the experiment? Or was a different set of participants tested in each condition? (See Chapters 2 and 3.) It's crucial from the point of statistical analysis for you to be absolutely clear about this, as different tests are appropriate in the two situations.

5. What was the dependent variable (the DV)?

What measure of performance was used in the experiment?

As with the IV, you can describe this at both more abstract and more concrete levels. For instance, the DV may be face-recognition performance, operationalised as the number of familiar faces correctly recognised. As with independent variables, it's perfectly possible to have more than one dependent variable. For example, in our face-recognition experiment, you could record the number of faces correctly recognised, the latency of a correct recognition response, and the number of false recognition responses.

6. Additional information.

Once you've given the basic structure of the experiment, outlined the variables and how they were operationalised, fill in any additional methodological information about the experiment that will not appear anywhere else. For example, in a within-subject design, you will have to consider how to balance the order of testing of conditions to avoid order effects (see Chapter 3). In between-subjects designs, allocation of subjects to different conditions needs to be considered (see Chapter 2). Perhaps the study involved matching participants in different conditions on some characteristic, or matching situational variables for pairs of participants in different conditions, or some other control measures. All these things relating to the general plan of the experiment can be included in this section.

<table>
<tr><td>

- Identify the independent variable.
- State how many values or levels it had.
- Describe how the IV and its levels were operationalised.
- Outline the type of design used.
- Describe the measure of performance, the DV.
- Give any other methodological details.

</td><td>

SUMMARY
Experimental design.

</td></tr>
</table>

Non-experimental studies.   Most students claim that the non-experimental studies are easier to understand than experimental designs but much more difficult to write up adequately. *"There doesn't seem to be much to say about the design"* is the usual worry. This may well be true, but there are *some* things you can say.

First, you have to recognise that you're dealing with a correlational study. A non-experimental study may be quite obviously a correlational study, with an explicit intention of exploring the relationship between two variables, e.g. the relationship between extroversion and performance on a vigilance task, with the data being analysed by a statistical test providing an index of correlation, such as Spearman's rho. Or the (co)relational structure may be a little deeper. For example, an analysis of the number of males and females succeeding or failing in some spatial task would constitute a correlational study in a conceptual sense, because it would be probing a possible relationship between gender and spatial ability.

In either case, the Design part of the study is somehow less tangible than in the case of true experiments. In fact the Design, the plan, *is* the actual attempt to examine the relationship between the variables. Let's see if we can develop a sequence of points to mention.

First, state the type of study it was; that is, a correlational one, its aim being to examine the relationship between two variables. Identify the variables. In some cases one of them may be considered to be the independent variable, in that it causes a change in the other, but it's probably simpler if you call it the *predictor* variable. For instance, in a study of the relationship between intelligence and examination performance, intelligence will be the *predictor* variable, examination performance the *predicted* variable. But in some cases both variables could be construed as dependent variables in that changes within them are presumably caused by some other variable within the subject, although you may not know what that is.

Finally, you could outline—just outline, for finer details can be reserved for the Procedure section—what happened in the experiment, and how measures of the two variables were obtained for each subject.

Participants (subjects)

It's important to provide information about the participants because they'll only be a small sample from the general population, and their particular characteristics may affect the extent to which it's possible to generalise your findings to the wider population. The information will also be relevant for possible replication of the study.

It's usual to give the following information:

i. The size of the sample, in total, and, if appropriate, numbers allocated to different conditions.
ii. Age (mean age, usually in years, and range), but, depending on what the experiment is investigating, much greater precision may be appropriate.
iii. Gender (perhaps linking this to the number of each).
iv. Occupation (which provides a rough guide to the educational level, and this may be relevant to the interpretations that can be drawn from your experiment).
iv. Manner of recruitment. Were participants volunteers, or was participation compulsory? Were they paid for partici-

pating? (Incidentally, avoid the phrase "Opportunity sample"; it doesn't feature in real scientific reports.)

    v.   Naiveté. Had the participants taken part in previous similar or other psychological experiments?

   vi.   Other details relevant to your specific experiment. For example, it may be important to indicate whether the participants' native language was English, if your experiment is to do with speed of word classification of unusual English words; or whether their vision was normal, if you were measuring visual thresholds.

Describe all the details in a paragraph of text, not in a list of separate points as here (see Chapter 9 for an example). Ethical considerations dictate that you respect others' privacy, and obtain only essential relevant information. It's unlikely, for instance, that a participant's home address will affect the number of words they remember from a list, although whether they happen to have had training in acting could well do so.

Materials

Apparatus. Specify any special apparatus that was used in the experiment for testing, stimulus presentation, or response recording, such as a video film or a piece of physiological equipment, stating its essential function and giving its make. There's no need to list everyday materials such as pen and paper. Many experiments are now computer-based, so give the type of computer used and briefly outline the basic features of the program in terms of its function, e.g. "displayed words for a controlled exposure duration". Full details of stimulus presentation can be given in the Procedure. In fact, in more advanced reports it's acceptable to slip details of common experimental equipment into the Procedure section, e.g. "An IBM 386 PC was used to present the visual stimuli, with the exposure duration set at 300msec. per stimulus and an inter-stimulus interval of two seconds."

Materials. Usually you can provide a lot of information about materials. Try not to be as brief as one student, who, with undeniable truth but a sad absence of feeling for detail, wrote "Words were used as stimuli". Don't forget that the aim of the Method section is to allow someone to *replicate* the experiment.

Sometimes it's useful to distinguish between "Materials", in the sense of specific tools used in conducting an experiment, such as questionnaires, and "Stimulus materials", in the sense of specific stimuli used in the experiment, having been selected from a wider range, and in this case this section could be labelled "Stimulus materials". In fact, don't be afraid to alter the title of this section to reflect your particular experiment. For example, if you had to construct novel stimuli, such as particular tunes or non-words that rhymed with real words, and stimulus presentation involved was technically complicated, an appropriate label might be "Stimulus construction and presentation".

In all cases describe the stimuli in as much detail as appropriate, with *relevant examples* in the text, and a complete listing in the Appendix. In the case of questionnaires, or other existing tests, give the name of the questionnaire or test and reference it in the Reference section if it is one that has been published, and, if you like, include a sample copy in the Appendix (but not in the main body of the report). If it's one that you've constructed yourself, then indicate this, without going into great detail of the technique of questionnaire construction and validation, (unless, of course, that happens to be the purpose of the study). Give details of its construction in a separate sub-section, or in the Appendix.

If stimuli had to be tested prior to the main experiment and adjusted in some way—for example, for audibility—describe this in this section.

Procedure

This is another black spot. *"I never know what to put into Design, and what into Procedure"* is a constant complaint. Try to think of the Design as something you could write before seeing how participants were tested, and the Procedure as a description of the actual process of testing.

An important point to start with in the case of between-subjects designs, if you haven't made it already in the Design section, is how participants were allocated to experimental conditions. (To avoid bias, this should be on a random basis.) Similarly, indicate the order of collecting the data in the different experimental conditions. This again should be randomised, and not one condition completed first before the other is started. Your behaviour or skill as an experimenter may change as you progress through the study, and you don't want a particular variant of your technique to be localised within one of the conditions.

Now you can move on to a detailed description of the Procedure. Think of it as a narrative account of moment-to-moment activity that took place during the experiment. It's as if you were giving a verbal commentary on a film or football match that only you can see. A useful approach is to describe the procedure for one subject in one particular experimental condition, and then give details of how the procedure varied for other conditions.

Here are a few additional points to mention:

- Was there any piloting of the procedure prior to the experiment proper, to iron out problems?
- How were instructions given? (verbally? written?) Give the instructions verbatim in the Appendix, but outline what they indicated to the participants in this section.
- Were participants given an opportunity to clarify any points?
- What was the rate of stimulus presentation? The inter-stimulus interval?
- What did the participant have to do? How did they indicate their responses?
- How were their responses recorded, measured?
- Was there an opportunity for correction of responses?
- Were practice trials given?
- How many test trials were there?
- Were participants given any feedback about their performance during testing?

Finally, describe the de-briefing session. Was the purpose of the experiment explained to participants? Were they given an opportunity to give introspective comments on any problems they experienced, or on how *they* perceived or construed the experimental task?

The Results section

The Results section contains two types of information: the actual results of the experiment, and the outcome of statistical analysis, or inferential statistics.

Presentation of data—tables

In general terms, everyone knows what "Results" mean, but exactly which aspects of the data you need to present in this section sometimes causes problems. Remember—your aim in this section is to allow your reader to gain an immediate appreciation of the *overall pattern* of findings in relation to the experimental aim, to examine at a glance any differences between conditions or relationships between variables.

So what you need is just a summary table of results, using descriptive statistics. This means that all data collected from individual participants on repeated test trials, from which your overall means are calculated, can't be presented here—there'd be far too much detail. These data—called the "raw" data because they haven't been collated, summarised or processed in any way—have to be relegated to the Appendix.

Start the section by giving a verbal description of the results, supported by a table of results. Refer your reader to the table in your verbal description. Your summary table should show the overall mean values for each condition, and some additional descriptive statistics, such as the standard deviation of scores. Make sure the table is formatted so that it is absolutely clear which parts of the data relate to which condition, and that the title specifies what the data represent (units of measurement). Look at Table 8.1. It contains a lot of information. It has a clear, comprehensible heading, which tells the reader what the experiment was about. The IV and DV can be deduced. It gives the units of measurement. It summarises the apparent effect of the IV, the difference between conditions, by giving the overall mean values per condition. It also provides an indication of the range, or variability, of scores; in other words, whether the apparent effect is due to just a small handful of participants behaving atypically in one of the conditions, or whether the effect of a particular type of processing is fairly consistent within each condition.

The data of Table 8.1 will have been derived from individual participants' scores, or raw data, as shown in Table 8.2. The individual participants' scores may not be completely "raw" themselves, of course, in that they may represent the mean of a number of trials undertaken by that participant. It's absolutely vital that a table such

	Condition 1 Shallow processing	Condition 2 Deep processing
Mean:	$X_1 \ldots$	$X_2 \ldots$
S.d.	$\ldots$	$\ldots$
$n_1 = \ldots, n_2 = \ldots$		

TABLE 8.1 Percentage of words correctly recalled following deep and shallow processing.

TABLE 8.2
Percentage of words correctly recalled by individual participants following deep and shallow processing. Each score represents the mean of two test trials.

Condition 1 Shallow processing	Condition 2 Deep processing
S1 —	S2 —
S3 —	S4 —
S5 —	S6 —
Sn —	Sn+1 —
Overall mean: X_1 —	
	X_2 —
S.d. —	—

as Table 8.2 appears somewhere in your report, as it forms an important part of the learning process. By indicating the distribution of participants across conditions, it illustrates the design of the experiment (in this case, a between-subjects design), so helping to clarify this concept, which is often difficult to grasp at first. It also provides information about individual differences in performance, which may form a useful discussion point later. However, it's not usual practice to include this level of detail in the main body of the Results section, so, unless your course requires otherwise, insert it into the Appendix, but indicate it in the main text as the source of the data in the main summary table.

Presentation of data—figures

An alternative way of presenting data would be in the form of a figure, usually a graph of some sort. This may be particularly valuable for displaying information from more than two conditions, or where items are the focus of attention, such as in serial position effects in memory experiments; or in correlational studies, where the relationship between two variables is being examined, and where a table would simply be a list of pairs of scores. A graph provides an immediate appreciation of the pattern of results, but, of course, loses out on the precision of information that is immediately available.

The graphical presentation of data may be in the form of a bar chart, line graph, pie chart and so on. It depends on the data you want to display. The most appropriate form for displaying the results of an experiment in which the levels of an IV differ qualitatively, e.g. emotional versus neutral words, is the bar chart or histogram. Remember to draw your graph so that the IV levels are indicated along the horizontal axis, the DV on the vertical axis. (These axes should only be called the "abscissa" and "ordinate", respectively, when they serve as lines of reference determining a position of a point.) Where both IV and DV are free to vary on a quantitative continuum, e.g. room temperature and reaction time, a line graph would be acceptable.

Graphical presentation of data is extremely useful for illustrating correlations (or lack of them) between two variables. In fact, it would be rather odd if you *didn't* present the data from a correlational study in the form of an x–y plot graph. Where there's an implicit assumption of the relationship between the variables being a directional one, it's logical to represent the predictor variable on the horizontal axis, the predicted variable on the vertical axis.

It's not usual in scientific reports to duplicate data by presenting them in both tabular and graphical form. However, it may sometimes be useful to do this in your report, particularly in a complex study where the essential effect is not immediately apparent from a table and can be more effectively illustrated by a graph. In this case include the graphical presentation in the Appendix.

Statistical analysis

The next stage is to show whether the particular pattern of results you've obtained is statistically significant—whether there is a real effect, or whether the pattern could have occurred by chance. That is, you'll want to report the results of applying inferential statistics to the data. You'll have learned from your statistics course which statistical tests are appropriate for particular experimental designs and types of data (parametric and non-parametric). In this part of the Results section you need to state how the data were analysed and what the outcome of that analysis was.

State clearly what statistical test was applied; give the value of the statistic calculated, and the degrees of freedom associated with it; state whether it was a one- or two-tailed test (depending on whether the original prediction was directional or not). Quote the probability level reached by the outcome of the analysis.

Give a verbal interpretation of the outcome of the analysis, both in general terms of supporting or failing to support the experimental prediction or hypothesis, and in more specific terms in relation to the actual content of the experiment.

Remember, NEVER say that the experimental hypothesis was proved. It can never be proved, because a single additional experiment may disprove it. It can only be *supported* by the experimental data. If the data support the experimental hypothesis, you can reject the null hypothesis. But if the data fail to support the experimental hypothesis, you *do not accept* the null hypothesis, because your study was not geared to examining any specific reason for an absence of a difference between conditions.

The verbal formula for describing the results of statistical analysis sometimes causes problems, so here's an example for a two-condition, within-subject experiment exploring time to fall asleep while listening to classical music or jazz, where the prediction of a difference was not directional:

> The data were analysed by related t test, which revealed a significant difference between the two conditions: $t\ 1, 11 = 6.47$, $P < 0.05$ (two-tailed test).
>
> Inspection of the means in Table X shows that it takes less time to fall asleep while listening to classical music than to jazz.

SUMMARY
Results section.

- Summarise the overall findings verbally.
- Present a summary of the results in a clearly and informatively formatted table, and/or:
- Present the data in graphical form.
- State how the data were analysed statistically with full details of the test and statistic.
- State the outcome of the analysis verbally, in relation to the experimental conditions.

The Discussion section

The Discussion section falls into several conceptual parts, but, as with the Introduction, they are not separately labelled. First, a statement of the findings, and what they mean in terms of the original aim. Second, an interpretation and critical assessment of the study and its findings. Third, a consideration of the implications of the findings for existing theory. Fourth, possible directions for further research.

Structuring the Discussion

The Discussion tends to progress from specific points to more general ones, going in the reverse direction to the Introduction. Start by describing the findings of the experiment, and what they show in relation to the original hypothesis, e.g. is face recognition affected by orientation of the face, and if so, in what precise way?

If your experiment failed to support the predicted outcome, then you'll have to search for possible reasons for the failure, looking at methodological inadequacies of the design or procedure, and discuss them here. Even if the findings are statistically significant, you need to consider whether this is a real effect stemming from the experimental manipulation, or whether there are alternative explanations of the results. So try to assess your experiment critically, as an outsider might, and anticipate and answer possible criticisms. You can act as a detective here, seeking possible hidden reasons for the observed pattern of results, and, once you've eliminated these, you may feel justified in accepting the results as they stand.

Once you can accept the results, discuss all the intricate details of the data, and try to interpret their meaning. Consider the implications of the findings for existing theory and research. Return to the themes of the Introduction, and show how the experiment relates to them. Are the findings in line with other research, or do they present a challenge to it? Do they confirm the prediction or do they require fresh explanations? Do they suggest a new theoretical model of some process, or have practical implications in some area? Finally, consider whether the experiment requires clarification or extension, or whether it suggests further research, and outline what this future research might entail.

The Conclusion

This is a brief statement summarising what the experiment has shown. It shouldn't be more than a sentence or so in length.

The Title, and the Abstract

Now that you've gone through the whole experiment and have a much clearer picture of what it entailed, you're ready to write the Abstract section.

This is a summary of the whole experiment, from its aims, even with allusion to its theoretical background, through what was done, what the findings were, to an interpretation of findings in relation to background research. But each of these aspects should be outlined in just a sentence or two, avoiding very specific details, so that the whole abstract is no more than a paragraph in length. (approximately 150–200 words).

The Title

This should be a single sentence (though two phrases separated by a colon are in order) serving as a unique identification of the experiment. It should inform the reader about the content, often indicating the variables involved, without going into unnecessary detail or using redundant phrases such as "An experiment to investigate …".

"Speed of face recognition as a function of orientation of the face" would be acceptable, but "Face recognition" or "An exploratory experiment to investigate if turning a face upside down makes it more or less difficult to recognise" would not.

References

In this section, list all the citations you've made in the text, in alphabetical order of the (first) author's name. Single publications by an author precede joint ones. Multiple publications by the same author should appear in chronological order. There's a fairly standard format for references of journal articles, so make sure that you pay attention to the minute details of punctuation, capital letters, and so on. It's fiddly, but well worth acquiring as a habit early on in your career.

Here's an example for a journal article:

Lukatela, G., & Turvey, M.T. (1990). Automatic and pre-lexical computation of phonology in visual word identification. *European Journal of Psychology*, 2, 325–343.

The surname of each author is followed by their initial(s), and 1990 is the date of publication. Then comes the title of the article, followed by the name of the journal in which it was published (underlined or in italics). The first number after the journal name indicates the volume number, followed by the (inclusive) page numbers.

Here's another example, for a reference to a book:

James, W. (1890). *Principles of psychology*. New York: Holt.

The order here is: author's surname; initial; date of publication; title of book; location and name of publishers.

Appendix section

Don't use this section as a junk box for everything you've accumulated during the experiment that can't be inserted into the main body of the report, but you can't bear to throw away. Make sensible use of the opportunity to give detailed information about aspects of the experiment that are too unwieldy and would detract from the essence of the report, but which are nevertheless important and may prove useful. Include such information as verbatim instructions, samples or complete lists of stimulus materials, questionnaires or other tests. The Appendix is also the home of raw data from which the summary data presented in the Results section are derived, and other aspects of data collation, such as histograms showing the distribution of scores.

Exercises

1. Write an imaginary abstract for the following experiments (you'll have to think a little bit about the possible experiment first):
   (a) The relationship between age and risk-taking behaviour.
   (b) The effect of smiling on subjective happiness.
   (c) The role of active versus passive exploration in learning a maze.

2. Re-write the following references in conventional style:
   (a) F. I. M. Craik, with R. S. Lockhart—article in the 11th volume of the journal of verbal learning and verbal behaviour in 1972, starting on page 671 and finishing on page 684, called levels of processing: a framework for memory research.

   (b) A book called reading, writing and dyslexia: a cognitive analysis, by Andrew Ellis, the second edition published by Lawrence Erlbaum Associates in 1993.

3. Allocate the following sentences to the Design or the Procedure sections:
   (a) Participants were told to press a key on hearing the tone.
   (b) The number of smiles was used as a measure of performance.
   (c) Two variables were manipulated in the study.
   (d) After presentation of a tune there was a silence of four seconds.
   (e) Administration of the drug involved a double-blind procedure.
   (f) Participants were matched on the basis of a pre-test for spelling ability.

Making sense of a journal article 9

John M. Gardiner

"Eighteen first year psychology students at Cardiff
acted as students".
"All the results were gathered together
and put on a table".
"The data were then *treated* to a test of significance".
"The results were *shockingly* non-significant".
"This result is clearly *wrong*".

Excerpts from an article in The Psychologist *(March, 1992) titled "Flashes
of brilliance" and consisting of a selection of statements from unattributed
(and unattributable) student essays (with emphasis added).*

Aims

This chapter aims to tell you a little about how research is
published and to guide you through reading one particular
article. There is therefore quite a lot of overlap between this
chapter and Chapter 8, but the emphasis differs, and so do the
objectives. At the end of this chapter you should have a much clearer
understanding of how to read articles critically and efficiently. The
particular article used for this purpose is republished here in full, but
accompanied by evaluative questions and exercises, and some
additional comments. The chapter concludes with some general rules
for reading journal articles.

Introduction

Science is a social enterprise. It depends on publication of results.
There is no point in having made an exciting discovery and not telling
anyone about it. So there have to be procedures for deciding which

results are sufficiently newsworthy and important to merit publication. Once results are published, then other scientists in the field can attempt to replicate them and follow them up, and in this way knowledge accumulates, develops, and is challenged. Much informal communication between scientists makes use of modern technology, particularly e-mail, and scientists often first present their results orally, in conference papers. But traditional journals remain the primary form of publication.

Most journals are published either by firms that specialise in academic publications, such as Academic Press or Psychology Press, or by professional organisations. Some organisations simply have their own house journal, such as the European Society for Cognitive Psychology, which publishes the *European Journal of Cognitive Psychology*, or the Experimental Psychology Society, which publishes the *Quarterly Journal of Experimental Psychology*. Others, particularly major national organisations, such as the American Psychological Association, the British Psychological Society, or the Psychonomic Society, publish a whole string of journals, most of which are devoted to particular specialist topics (e.g. *Memory & Cognition, Psychobiology*).

All journals have an editor, who will be a leading expert in the field, and an editorial board, which may include associate editors, who are normally appointed by the editor on the strength of their reputation in research. The fundamental principle that determines publication is that of *peer review*. The hopeful author prepares a manuscript that conforms to the requirements stipulated by the journal, then submits it to the editor with a cover letter that might go something like this:

> Dear Dr. Ebbinghaus,
> I enclose five copies of a manuscript entitled "Forgetting and reconstructive memory" that I would like to submit for publication in *Memory*.
> Yours sincerely,
> Frederic Bartlett

Not so very long ago it was not uncommon for editors to deal directly with a submitted manuscript, and the optimistic author might look forward to receiving a reply along the following lines:

> Dear Dr. Bartlett,
> Thank you very much for submitting your most interesting paper to *Memory*. I wish I'd thought of that myself. I am

happy to accept your paper for publication and it will
appear in the November issue of the journal.
Yours sincerely,
Hermann Ebbinghaus

However, such a procedure is obviously open to abuse, which is
one reason why nowadays such editorial action is very rare. (There
are stories of one journal editor who used to submit, and accept for
publication, manuscripts he had written himself, under a
pseudonym.) Usually, the editor will send out two or three copies of
the submitted manuscript to other experts on the topic, typically
including at least one member of the editorial board. These referees or
reviewers send the editor a detailed critique, and they often have to
complete a checklist of recommendations too. The checklist is for the
editor's sole use. The editor then sends all the reviews to the author,
together with an action letter explaining to the author exactly how the
paper needs to be revised before it can be accepted for publication. If
the reviews are particularly negative, the paper may simply be
rejected at this stage. The editor also sends copies of the action letter
to all the reviewers, together with copies of the other reviews. The
action letter and each review may sometimes run to three or more
single spaced pages. (It is not entirely unknown for the action letter
and reviews to exceed the length of the submitted manuscript.) The
author now has to revise the paper in the light of all the comments
made about it, and resubmit it, together with a detailed cover letter
explaining all the changes made, and also explaining where changes
have not been made, if he or she disagrees with some of the comments.
The editor may accept the revision, or send it out for further review,
then back for further revision. Even after that, the paper may still be
rejected, although good editors will try to reject unsuitable papers at
an earlier stage.

Responsible authors do not submit work that is obviously flawed in
any way, because of some error in design, say, or some weakness in the
data, such as ceiling or floor effects. So peer review usually results in
rejection for other reasons, generally to do with a judgement as to whether
the paper makes a significant—theoretically or empirically significant,
not statistically—contribution to knowledge. Reputable journals set high
publication standards, and their rejection rates (the proportion of
submissions not accepted for publication) are sometimes as high as 70%
or 80%. Roughly speaking, the more reputable the journal in which
authors publish their work, the more likely it is that their work will
command the attention and interest of others in the field.

But authors usually have a pretty good idea of how their work is likely to be regarded by their peers. And so they will usually bear that in mind when choosing the journal to which they first submit their paper. Most scientists in the field would broadly agree on a "pecking order" of journals, going from the most desirable one to be published in, to the least desirable (and even journals completely to be avoided, if one wishes to retain a good scientific reputation). So there is also a large element of self-evaluation, was well as peer review.

A lot of research is never published. It ends up in the back of filing cabinets. And usually soon afterwards the Freudian mechanism of repression is successfully invoked. (Experienced scientists occasionally find themselves getting quite excited about interesting ideas for new experiments, only to realise much later, and after considerable thought, that they did those experiments some years ago, and the experiments hadn't produced publishable results.)

Structure of an article

All journal articles are divided into sections. The main sections are the abstract, the introduction, the method, the results, and the discussion. Some of these sections are subdivided further, especially the method section. Sometimes there are additional main sections, where more than one experiment is described. Sometimes results and discussion sections are combined. And sometimes there is a general discussion section or conclusion. The main sections—the introduction, method, results, and discussion—should tell the reader *why the research was done, how it was done, what happened,* and *what should be made of it* (at least, in the opinion of the authors).

The title and the abstract are very important, and may often determine whether the reader reads any further. Titles are as brief but informative as possible, and redundant words like "A study of …", "An investigation of …" or "Experiments on …" are to be avoided. Often a title says what has been varied and what has been measured. Sometimes it encapsulates the main news—it says what has been found. Usually, underneath the title the names of the authors appear, together with their affiliation (the place that employs them).

The abstract, which is restricted in length (typically to 120, 150, or 200 words, depending on the journal) gives a succinct summary of the entire article. It does this in such a way as to stand completely alone, and to enable any potential reader to decide whether the article itself is of sufficient interest to bother with. This is where readers are won or lost (if they weren't put off by the title). Abstracts are also published separately in various databases (e.g. *Psychological Abstracts*), which can scanned, and indexed, and classified.

The introduction motivates the research. It provides a summary, if not a detailed review, of previous relevant work. It explains what is to be learned from the research that is to be described. It makes clear what question or questions the research addresses, and why this question or questions are interesting and important.

The method gives a full and precise account of the way the research was done. The main aim of this section is to enable other researchers to attempt a direct replication of the experiment—that is, to do it again in exactly the same way—if they want to. This section also allows critics who think they could have done the research better to figure out exactly how they could have improved on the method the authors used.

The results section presents the results, in summary form, often graphically or in a table, and it describes them. It also summarises the outcome of any inferential (as opposed to descriptive) statistics. This section tells the reader what happened in the data, and how the actual outcome compares with the expected outcome.

The discussion usually reminds the reader of the question or questions the research set out to answer, and restates the main findings. It then explains what the authors make of these findings; that is, what they think the theoretical (or practical) significance of the results might be. Many authors seem unable to resist writing lengthy discussions, presumably under the misapprehension that length and importance are correlated positively. Editors might do more to discourage this habit. But, unfortunately, lengthy discussion is partly a consequence of peer review—all those critics whose comments have to be taken on board. At the end of the discussion (the longer it is, the more it can be skipped), the reader should come away able to say what has been learned from the article, preferably in a sentence or two.

Other parts of an article include references, listed separately at the end, footnotes, including author notes on the first page, and sometimes an appendix. At the very end of the article, it is usual to state the dates on which the original manuscript was submitted and the paper accepted for publication.

SUMMARY

- Publication in reputable journals is decided by editors acting on the basis of reviews from other experts on the topic of the research.
- The guiding principle is known as peer review—rejection rates are quite high, in the more prestigious journals, and articles that are accepted usually have first to be revised.
- Articles have to conform to certain general conventions regarding their structure.
- Each section of an article has a particular purpose, and the overall goal of the sections is to facilitate scientific communication.

Introduction to the sample article

The rest of this chapter takes you through one journal article and provides guidelines about what to look out for in trying to evaluate it. The article is about an effect in memory called "the generation effect". This effect occurs when two study conditions are compared, one in which subjects simply read whatever it is they are asked to memorise, the other in which they have to generate whatever it is they are asked to memorise. For example, they might read or generate a set of opposites (e.g. up DOWN, short ——?, dark ——?, thin FAT). In this case, the generation effect would be finding that subjects were subsequently more likely to recognise or recall the opposites that they had generated than the opposites that they had read. This effect is intriguing theoretically, and—on the assumption that generating involves more work than reading—satisfying ethically, at least from a Protestant standpoint.

There were several reasons for choosing this particular article. It is brief. The experiments are conceptually simple. The basic effect can easily be replicated in an undergraduate laboratory. The experiments were actually done by an undergraduate as part of a final year project. And, as the article is one of my own publications, there is no possibility of offending anyone else by any critical remarks I make about it now.

The article was published in *Memory & Cognition* in 1984. It is reproduced in full, by kind permission of the owners of the copyright, the original publishers, the Psychonomic Society. Questions, exercises and comments have been interpolated in the original text.

A generation effect with numbers rather than words

JOHN M. GARDINER and JEAN M.C. ROWLEY*

The City University, London, England

It has previously been shown that a word from a list is more likely to be remembered if the word was generated, rather than read, by the subject. Two simple experiments that show that a similar generation effect occurs in remembering answers to multiplication sums are described. It is suggested that this finding is inconsistent with a strong version of a lexical activation hypothesis that had been proposed to account for the generation effect. According to that hypothesis, the generation effect is due to enhanced activation of the semantic features of a word's representation in the subjective lexicon.

In a series of recent studies, Slamecka and his colleagues have shown that a word from a list is more likely to be remembered if it is generated, rather than read, by the subject (McElroy & Slamecka, 1982; Slamecka & Fevreiski, 1983; Slamecka & Graf, 1978; see, too, Jacoby, 1978, 1983). This phenomenon—the generation effect—has been found to occur in both recall and recognition memory tests, and to be quite uninfluenced by the rule or context provided for generate and read tasks (Slamecka & Graf, 1978; see, too, Gardiner & Arthurs, 1982). It has also been found, however, that the type of item generated is critical, for the effect has been shown not to occur with nonwords (McElroy & Slamecka, 1982). This finding led McElroy and Slamecka to infer that involvement of semantic memory is a necessary condition for the generation effect, and to propose the more specific hypothesis that the effect is due to enhanced activation of semantic features of a word's representation in the subjective lexicon. As Slamecka and Fevreiski (1983) put it, "generation will have functional consequences only if the generated unit already has representation in the subjective lexicon. That is, the generational product must be a word in one's vocabulary, and therefore must possess semantic attributes" (p. 161).

This interpretation gained additional support from the results of Slamecka and Fevreiski's (1983) study, which showed that subjects' attempts to generate the required words need not be successful for a generation effect to occur (see, too, Gardiner, Craik, & Bleasdale, 1973), and also from Jacoby's (1983) elegant demonstration that, although generated words were better remembered in a test of recognition memory, in a visual-perception identification task it was the read words that were more likely to be identified. Thus, generating the surface features of the required word was not critical, and, for an identification task in which surface features were at a premium, reading was actually more advantageous than generating. It seems clear, therefore, that the semantic features of a word, as opposed to its surface features, give rise to the generation effect.

The lexical activation hypothesis proposed by McElroy and Slamecka (1982) strongly suggests a need for further evidence on the generality of the effect with respect to the type of item used; the question of whether there are kinds of item other than words that might produce an effect has an obvious bearing on the hypothesis. For example, the hypothesis would be further confirmed were it to be shown that no generation effect occurs when numerical items are used in the context of some arithmetic operation, such as multiplication. On the other hand, were it to be shown that such numbers do give rise to a generation effect, then the lexical activation hypothesis would be rejected—at least as presently formulated. (It would, of course, be possible to fall back on some weaker version of the hypothesis, and reject only the strong version.) There appears to be little evidence available on the question of whether or not a generation effect does occur with numerical items; hence, we describe two simple experiments that were designed to provide such evidence[1].

* We thank James A. Hampton for helpful suggestions. A preliminary report of these experiments was included in a paper given by John M. Gardiner and James A. Hampton at the London Conference of the British Psychological Society, December 1983. The authors' mailing address is: Division of Psychology, The City University, Northampton Square, London EC1V 4PB, England.

Questions and exercises

1. How well does the abstract summarise the article, in so far as you could tell, without having read further?
2. How well does the introduction explain the background to the problem that the experiments address?
3. Can you in your own words briefly describe what the generation effect is, and how the lexical activation hypothesis explains it?
4. Can you say how the authors propose to test this hypothesis?
5. Does the test they propose seem a reasonable one? How else might the hypothesis be tested?
6. What are the possible outcomes of the experiments, and what would each outcome mean for the hypothesis?

Comments

It might strike you that the lexical activation hypothesis was taken a little too literally—numbers are also words, after all, and therefore have some semantic attributes. The theoretical motivation for the experiments seems weak. However, at least the empirical point is clear. Either there will be a generation effect with numbers, or there won't be.

EXPERIMENT 1

In Experiment 1, the subjects studied a list that consisted of familiar multiplication sums. Half of the sums were presented in a generate task, that is, without the answers, and half were presented in a read task, that is, with the answers. Afterwards, the subjects were given a recognition memory test for the answers to all the sums from the list.

Method

Design. The design had one within-subjects variable: task (generate vs. read). All subjects studied a single list of 20 multiplication sums; 10 of the answers were generated, and 10 were read. They were then given two successive recognition tests in which they had to identify those answers from among other, lure answers to similar multiplication sums. The first test was a free-choice test in which they were instructed not to guess; the second was a forced-choice test.

Materials. From the 2-times multiplication table up to the 12-times multiplication table there are 40 two-digit answers, excluding 10 and 12. These 40 numbers were divided arbitrarily into two equal sets, one for use in the study list and one for use in the recognition test as lures. For any subset of answers all beginning with the same digit, list items and lures were divided as evenly as possible. For example, of the 7 answers that fall within the 20 to 29 range, 4 served as target responses and 3 as lures. Multiplication sums were then chosen for each target response in such a way that nine of the multiplication tables were used twice and two once.

Procedure. The list items were presented as numbers on cards at the rate of 4 sec each. For 10 of the items, the answer to the sum was shown, and for the other 10, a question mark was shown instead (e.g., $9 \times 4 = 36$; $8 \times 5 = ?$). Generate items for half the subjects were read items for the other half, and the task was blocked such that half the subjects began with generate items and half with read items. Within each block, the sums were randomly reordered for each subject. The subjects had to say aloud both the sum and its answer in both generate and read conditions. They were told that subsequently their memory for the answers to those particular sums would be tested. In order to reduce performance levels somewhat, a free-association test was interpolated between the study list and the recognition tests. In this test, the experimenter read out a series of 30 stimulus words, 1 word at a time, and the subjects had to respond rapidly by saying aloud the first word they thought of in connection with each stimulus. The recognition tests were then administered. They were presented on a single sheet on which the 20 target numbers and the 20 lure numbers were randomly mixed together. In the first test, the subjects were instructed to work carefully down each column without backtracking and to circle any numbers that they felt sure were answers to the sums they had called out earlier. After completing this test, they were told that, in fact, 20 of the 40 numbers on the sheet were answers to those sums and that, using a pen of a different color, they were to continue selecting targets until they had selected up to a total of 20, if necessary making just the best guesses they could.

Subjects. The subjects were 24 undergraduate students at The City University, London, who volunteered to participate in the experiment without pay. They were tested individually. Two subjects unaccountably experienced some difficulty with the generation task and were replaced.

Questions and exercises

1. Is the experiment described precisely enough for you to be able to reconstruct it? If you wanted to do a direct replication—to repeat the experiment exactly—is all the information you need provided?

2. Can you define the independent and dependent variables?

3. Was the experiment done right? Are there any flaws in the design and procedure?

4. How else might the experiment have been designed? What other possibilities are there? Can you think of a better way of doing it?

Comments

The most important methodological point is that the *sole* difference between generate and read study conditions (the independent variable) is whether the numbers were generated or read. This is why all other conditions were held constant, or counterbalanced, including most especially the actual numbers involved. Other important issues are whether enough people were tested, and whether they were given enough numbers to generate or read. Rules of thumb typically determine such decisions, which are quite arbitrary. So are other decisions, such as the choice of a multiplication task (it might have been division, addition, or subtraction), and the choice of test, which was recognition (the dependent variable). Other procedural details, such as the presentation rate for the study list, simply reflect established practice in similar previous experiments.

The second of the two successive recognition tests was not really necessary. But it does make an additional point, because it is a forced-choice test—participants were forced to choose the correct number of items, 20. In the first test, in which they were free to decide how many test items to choose, different response criteria might be involved. For example, in the free-choice test people might be less likely to choose read items than generate items because they were less sure about them.

Results and discussion

The probability of a false-positive response in the initial, free-choice test was .07. Recognition probabilities for each recognition test are shown in Figure 1, from which it is obvious that there is superior recognition following the generate task. The results of two separate ANOVAs carried out on the number of words correctly recognised by each subject showed that the generation effect was highly significant in both the free-choice test [$F(1,23) = 49.09$, $MSe = 2.22$, $p < .001$ and the forced-choice test [$F(1,23) = 35.56$, $MSe = 1.35$, $p < .001$]. Thus, at least so far as recognition memory is concerned, there is a generation effect with these numbers comparable to that previously obtained with words.

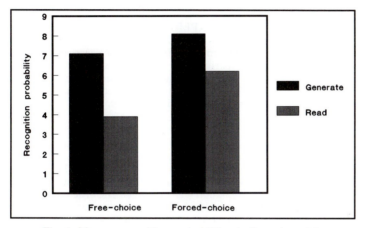

Fig. 1. Mean recognition probabilities in Experiment 1.

Comments

The generation effect appears to be larger in the free-choice test than in the forced-choice test. But performance was very high for the generate items in the forced-choice test. There was probably a ceiling effect—some people probably recognised all or nearly all these items. As no one can improve on 100% correct, this means that those participants might have shown a larger generation effect, had they been able to do so. But it doesn't matter, because the size of the effect in each test is not relevant to the hypothesis. The hypothesis is merely that there will be a generation effect. The ceiling effect actually works against this hypothesis. So although one tries to avoid ceiling effects, they aren't necessarily always A BAD THING. It depends on whether or not they compromise the conclusions one wants to draw from the experiment.

Questions and exercises

1. What was the main result, and were the conclusions drawn from this result reasonable?

2. Are there any problems in the data, and in the data analyses, with respect to those conclusions?

3. How do the actual outcomes of the experiment compare with the expected outcomes, and what does this mean for the hypothesis?

EXPERIMENT 2

In Experiment 2, the subjects studied the same list of multiplication sums, and again, half of the sums were presented in a generate task and half in a read task. Experiment 2, however, involved multitrial free-recall learning, for it was designed to investigate the possibility that, unlike the generation effect with words, a generation effect with numbers might occur only in recognition memory.

Method

Design and procedure. The design was a 2 × 3 factorial with task (generate vs. read) and trials (1-3) both as within-subjects factors. Apart from the use of free-recall learning, in most other respects Experiment 2 was essentially identical to Experiment 1, for the list items and their manner and rate of presentation were the same. The ordering of items within each generate and read block was varied across trials. A different free-association test, reduced from 30 to 20 stimulus words, was given immediately after each study trial and before recall. The recall tests were written and terminated by the subjects. The next study trial then began immediately. On a very few occasions on the first trial, a subject failed to generate the answer to the sum within 4 sec; when that happened, the answer was given before the next sum was presented.

Subjects. The subjects were 24 students at The City University, London, who volunteered to participate in the experiment without pay. They were tested individually.

Comments

There was no new theoretical point to be made by this experiment. The important point was to see if the results are replicable. If they could not be replicated in a recall test, a test in which generation effects are found with words, then there would be something odd about the effect with numbers. It could not then be argued that the effect with numbers is like the effect with words, And this difference would have to be explained. Moreover, one would then want to replicate Experiment 1 directly, to be sure that the effect in recognition is real.

This experiment involved several opportunities to study and recall the items. So the experiment introduced a second independent variable, the number of trials, and a different dependent variable, recall. Similar questions and exercises apply to this experiment as to the previous experiment, so they haven't been repeated here.

Results and discussion

The recall probabilities are shown in Figure 2, from which it can be seen that recall is markedly superior following the generate task. The results of an ANOVA carried out on the number of words recalled by each subject revealed a highly significant generation effect [$F(1,23) = 36.78$, MSe = 3.29, p < .001, as well as a highly significant effect of trials [$F(2,46)$ = 90.48, MSe = 0.66, p < .001]. The interaction was not significant [$F(2,46)$ = 2.61, MSe = 0.87]. The results of this experiment therefore show that a generation effect with numbers may be obtained as readily with multitrial free-recall learning as with recognition memory testing.

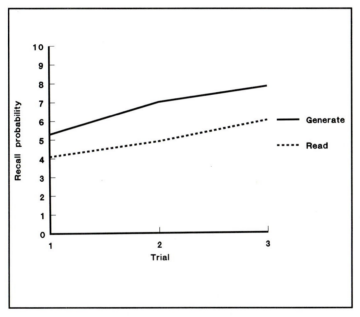

Fig. 2.   Mean free-recall probabilities in Experiment 2.

Comments

The generation effect was similar across all three trials in this experiment. There is no indication that the effect was becoming larger, or smaller, from one trial to the next. This was just as well, because there was no reason to expect such differences. Had such differences occurred, there would have been no ready explanation of them. In statistical terms, this means that the effects of study condition and of trials were *additive*. The two independent variables did not influence each other. When two independent variables do influence each other significantly (as would have happened if the generation effect was becoming smaller or larger across trials), this kind of effect is described as an *interaction*.

CONCLUSIONS

The results of this study demonstrate that a similar generation effect occurs in remembering numbers from multiplication tables to that found previously in remembering words from a word list. This outcome seems inconsistent with the lexical activation hypothesis proposed by McElroy and Slamecka (1982). According to that hypothesis, the generation effect is due to enhanced activation of the semantic features of a word's representation in the subjective lexicon.

Of course, although largely devoid of semantic attributes, numbers will undoubtedly be assumed to be represented in the subjective lexicon by many theorists, and so it remains quite possible to retain some weaker version of the lexical activation hypothesis, despite the existence of a generation effect with numbers. However, the lexical activation hypothesis was, in our view, prematurely specific, and we prefer to argue for a broader view. Although agreeing with McElroy and Slamecka (1982) that semantic memory involvement seems to be a necessary condition for the generation effect, we suggest in contrast that any type of item at all may give rise to a generation effect, provided only that it activates some existing representation in some knowledge system in semantic memory. Perhaps the point is more aptly expressed in a caveat by Kintsch (1980), who warned that "attempts to equate semantic memory with word meanings only, that is, with the 'subjective lexicon', are misguided and doomed to failure. Semantic memory is our whole-world knowledge—including what we know about robins, $7 \times 4 = 28$, what to do in a restaurant, and the history of the Civil War, to cite some prominent examples" (p.596).

Questions and exercises

1. Have the authors reasonably summarised the experimental results?
2. Have they adequately discussed their findings in relation to the hypothesis they were testing?
3. Are there other implications they seem to have overlooked, and other ways of interpreting their results?

Comments

Far from going on at great length, these authors didn't have much to say about their results. This probably reflects the lack of any strong theoretical motivation for the experiments. The main point seemed to be simply that generation effects occur with numbers, as well as with words, pretty much as promised by the title of the article.

Theoretically, the suggestion is that any kind of item might give rise to a generation effect, provided people have come across the item before—this is what is meant by the item being represented in some knowledge system in semantic memory. Other researchers later went on to disprove this hypothesis by showing that under certain conditions quite novel items, such as nonwords, can give rise to a generation effect (e.g. Johns & Swanson, 1988; Nairne & Widner, 1987).

But the broader question of the generality of any particular phenomenon is important. It is necessary to establish the boundary conditions of a phenomenon, partly to understand it theoretically, partly to appreciate its practical implications. For example, do generation effects occur in everyday life, outside laboratories? Might such effects be used to enhance learning, in education? Such questions continue to be of interest. For a recent article about this, see "A generation effect can be found during naturalistic learning", by Patricia DeWinstanley (1995).

REFERENCES

GARDINER, J.M., & ARTHURS, F.S. (1982). Encoding context and the generation effect multitrial free-recall learning. *Canadian Journal of Psychology, 36,* 527–531.

GARDINER, J.M., CRAIK, F.I.M., & BLEASDALE, F.A. (1973). Retrieval difficulty and subsequent recall. *Memory & Cognition, 1,* 213–216.

JACOBY, L.L. (1978). On interpreting the effects of repetition: Solving a problem versus remembering a solution. *Journal of Verbal Learning and Verbal Behavior, 17,* 649–667.

JACOBY, L.L. (1983). Remembering the data: Analysing interactive processes in reading. *Journal of Verbal Learning and Verbal Behavior, 22,* 485–508.

KINTSCH, W. (1980). Semantic memory: A tutorial. In R.S. Nickerson (Ed.), *Attention and performance VIII.* Hillsdale, NJ: Erlbaum.

McELROY, L.A., & SLAMECKA, N.J. (1982). Memorial consequences of generating nonwords: Implications for semantic-memory interpretations of the generation effect. *Journal of Verbal Learning and Verbal Behavior, 21,* 249–259.

RUSSO, J.E., & WISHER, R.A. (1976). Reprocessing as a recognition cue. *Memory & Cognition, 4,* 683–689.

SLAMECKA, N.J., & FEVREISKI, J. (1983). The generation effect when generation fails. *Journal of Verbal Learning and Verbal Behavior, 22,* 153–163.

SLAMECKA, N.J., & GRAF, P. (1978). The generation effect: Delineation of a phenomenon. *Journal of Experimental Psychology: Human Learning and Memory, 4,* 592–604.

NOTE

1. There is some evidence indicating superior recognition of internally generated numbers (e.g. Russo & Wisher, 1976).

(Manuscript received March 15, 1984; revision accepted for publication May 24, 1984.)

Final comments

The way the references are cited follows the conventions of most publications in the field. The note acknowledges that other researchers had done closely related research, a fact brought to the attention of the authors by someone whose scholarship with respect to the literature exceeded theirs—Norman Slamecka, one of the reviewers that the then editor of *Memory & Cognition*, Robert Bjork, had asked to referee the submission. It was the Slamecka and Graf (1978) article that had—to paraphrase their title—delineated the phenomenon, and launched a revival of interest in it.

Final exercises

A useful exercise after reading any paper is to try to say in your own words (and as few words as possible) what the authors did, what they found, and what they made of it. So, for example: "These guys found a generation effect in memory for numbers, answers to multiplication sums. They argued this finding discredits a strong version of a lexical activation hypothesis, according to which the effect occurs only for words. They suggested that perhaps any familiar kind of item will produce the generation effect".

A second useful exercise is to think about how the research might be followed up. Suppose you wanted to do an experiment that followed up the ones you've just read about. What other experiments are suggested? Even what might seem to be routine extensions of previous work are important in providing evidence about the generality of an effect. For example, does the generation effect for numbers depend on the numerical task? Would it matter if people did division, instead of multiplication? Does the effect depend on the kind of numbers generated? Would it work for unfamiliar sequences of numbers like 3,5,6,2,1,7? (For some relevant evidence, and another example of how the Gardiner and Rowley paper was followed up, see Gardiner & Hampton, 1985). And so on. New experiments rarely involve a great imaginative leap. They are often quite modest extensions of previous experiments. Scientific knowledge typically accrues by small increments—brick by brick.

SUMMARY

- This article described two experiments that aimed to test the generality of a particular phenomenon, the generation effect.
- The experiments showed that this effect occurs with numbers, an outcome that has implications for hypotheses about the cause of the effect particularly the lexical activation hypothesis.
- The most important thing in reading the article is to ask critical questions.

General rules for reading journal articles

Journal articles are written in quite technical language. The intended readership is other researchers, rather than undergraduate students. This can make them pretty tough going. This final part of the chapter provides six general rules for reading journal articles. These rules should help.

Rule 1. *Read the abstract first*. And read it thoroughly. Try to gain from it a clear view of what the article is going to be about and whether it is going to be of interest to you.

Rule 2. *Skip difficult sections*. Extract the gist. It usually isn't important to understand everything the authors say. Authors may spend many hours honing their words. But that doesn't place you under any obligation. Treat authors brusquely.

Rule 3. *Read with particular goals in mind*. The main goal is to be able to understand in broad terms what the authors did, what they found, and what they made of their findings. Try to come away from reading an article able to tell someone who has not read it those three main points.

Rule 4. *Ask critical questions*. Bear in mind the kinds of critical questions that were interpolated in the text of the article you have just read. Don't just accept what you read: evaluate it.

Rule 5. *Be creative*. Try to think of other ways of testing the hypothesis, and other interpretations of the results. Try to relate the results to other findings, and other ideas, that you have read about elsewhere. Think of other theoretical implications, and new experiments.

Rule 6. *Persevere.* Reading journal articles is never going to be as easy as reading newspaper articles. But, like most skills, it will improve with practice. So keep trying. The ultimate reward is becoming able to understand research for yourself, instead of having to rely on secondary sources like conventional text books to explain it to you.

And three final tips

It is rarely necessary to study any article in detail. There are altogether far too many articles, and there isn't enough time. (Researchers themselves find it almost impossible to "keep up with the literature", even in their own quite narrowly defined fields of interest). Probably the only articles you will need to study in any detail are those you intend to use as the basis for some new research, particularly if the research is to be closely modelled on that described in the article. Only then do you really need to pore through method sections, in order to try to figure out exactly how the research was done. Otherwise, don't bother.

As for statistics, don't bother much either (unless you want to). The results of inferential statistics (mostly analyses of variance, or ANOVAs) are often presented at considerable length. If the article is published in a reputable journal, you can usually take it for granted that the statistical results support the stated conclusions, just as you can usually take it for granted that the experiments will have no obvious methodological flaws. And the more important scientific issue is whether the results of experiments are replicable. Statistical results represent merely a probabilistic guess at replicability. They estimate how likely it is that the outcome is a fluke. The only way to be sure it isn't a fluke is to replicate it. Scientifically speaking, then, statistics are not significant. The significant thing is the science.

In 1979 a famous scientist, Sir Peter Medawar, published a small classic called *Advice to a young scientist*. It is full of useful tips for any scientist, or would-be scientist, young or old. The third and last tip is taken from that book. Here are some excerpts from what Peter Medawar had to say about reading:

> Too much book learning may crab and confine the imagi-
> nation, and endless poring over the research of others is
> sometimes psychologically a research substitute, much as

reading romantic fiction may be a substitute for real-life romance. ... The beginner *must* read, but intently and choosily and not too much. Few sights are sadder than that of a young research worker always to be seen hunched over journals in the library; by far the best way to become proficient in research is to get on with it ...

References

DeWinstanley, P.A. (1995). A generation effect can be found during naturalistic learning. *Psychonomic Bulletin & Review, 2,* 538–541.

Gardiner, J.M., & Hampton, J.A. (1985). Semantic memory and the generation effect: Some tests of the lexical activation hypothesis. *Journal of Experimental Psychology: Learning, Memory, and Cognition, 11,* 732–741.

Johns, E.E., & Swanson, L.G. (1988). The generation effect with nonwords. *Journal of Experimental Psychology: Learning, Memory, and Cognition, 14,* 180–190.

Medawar, P.B. (1979). *Advice to a young scientist*. London: Harper & Row.

Nairne, J.S., & Widner, R.L. (1987). Generation effects with nonwords: The role of test appropriateness. *Journal of Experimental Psychology: Learning, Memory, and Cognition, 13,* 164–171.

Slamecka, N.J., & Graf, P. (1978). The generation effect: Delineation of a phenomenon. *Journal of Experimental Psychology: Human Learning and Memory, 4,* 592–604.

Author index

Subject index

Personality theory and astrology 2–3, 13
Physical situation 111–112
Physiological situation 108–109
Pilot experiments 34, 35, 37
Placebos 105, 106, 118
Post hoc explanation 18
Power *see* Statistical power
Practice effects 47–48, 49
Pre-test/post-test designs 43–44
Prediction 18, 19, 139–140, 144
Privacy 119, 120, 126, 145
Protection from harm 125, 127
Psychometric tests 24, 66, 74
Psychophysical studies 42–43

Quasi-experimental variables 28–29
Questionnaires
  analysis 68, 69
  data collection methods 80–83
  functions 73–75
  group-administered 80–81, 82–83
  interviews 81–82
  layout 88–91
  postal 81
  quality evaluation 91–95
  question content 76–77
  question types 83–86, 90
  question wording 86–88
  reliability assessment 91–93
  report writing 146
  respondents 77–79
  self-administered 80
  specifications 75–76
  validity assessment 93–95

Random allocation 60–61
Random sampling 100
Randomisation 27, 53–54
Range effects 29–30, 35, 56, 165
'Real world'
  application 8–10
  avoidance 10–11

correlational studies 64–65
  pre-test/post-test designs 43–44
References 136–137, 153
Repeated measures design *see*
  Within-subjects designs
Research
  acquiring knowledge 5–7
  basic tools 97–99
  case study 104
  strategies 67

Science
  development of method 16–19
  education 4–5
  psychology as a 3–5, 20
Scientific writing *see* Journal articles;
  Writing reports
Signal detection theory 10
Significance level 31, 34
Situations *see* Physical situation;
  Physiological situation; Social
  situation
Social situation 109–111
Software programs, statistical 17
Statistical measurement 30–31
  and causality 62–63
  interpreting results 32
  report writing 150–151
  see also Data
Statistical
  and experimental design 32–35, 109
  homogenous groups 101
  power 31–32
  within-subject designs 45
Students, expectations of 1–3, 6–7, 11
Subjects
  as own control 45
  dropout 49, 50
  numbers 45–46
  recruitment of 99–103
  report writing 144–145
  see also Questionnaires, respondents